"A penetrating look at how to break the cycle of child abuse in today's world." —*Moving Worlds*

"Miller is both prolific . . . and eloquent in her continuing indictment of parents who abuse their children and societies that tolerate such behavior." —*Kirkus Reviews*

"What Miller has to say is enlightening. . . . This is not a book that can be read through once and put aside. The reader can return again and again as new truth is recognized." —*South Bend, Indiana, Tribune*

"She is passionate, human, and in many ways helpful in her attacks on the media, the clergy, and her own profession." —*Christian Century*

"Miller charts valuable territory." —*New Age Journal*

"A moving argument for awareness and condemnation of child abuse." —*Science News*

ALICE MILLER has been a practicing psychotherapist for over twenty-five years and is the author of bestselling books on child abuse and its effects, including the classic *The Drama of the Gifted Child* and *Thou Shalt Not Be Aware* (available in a Meridian edition).

OTHER BOOKS BY ALICE MILLER

The Drama of the Gifted Child
(originally published as
Prisoners of Childhood)

For Your Own Good: Hidden Cruelty in Childrearing and the Roots of Violence

Thou Shalt Not Be Aware: Society's Betrayal of the Child

Pictures of a Childhood: Sixty-six Watercolors and an Essay

The Untouched Key: Tracing Childhood Trauma in Creativity and Destructiveness

Banished Knowledge: Facing Childhood Injuries

ALICE MILLER

Breaking Down the Wall of Silence

The Liberating Experience of Facing Painful Truth

Translation by Simon Worrall

Revised Edition

With a New Preface by the Author

A MERIDIAN BOOK

MERIDIAN
Published by the Penguin Group
Penguin Books USA Inc., 375 Hudson Street, New York, New York 10014, U.S.A.
Penguin Books Ltd, 27 Wrights Lane, London W8 5TZ, England
Penguin Books Australia Ltd, Ringwood, Victoria, Australia
Penguin Books Canada Ltd, 10 Alcorn Avenue, Toronto, Ontario, Canada M4V 3B2
Penguin Books (N.Z.) Ltd, 182–190 Wairau Road, Auckland 10, New Zealand

Penguin Books Ltd, Registered Offices:
Harmondsworth, Middlesex, England

Published by Meridian, an imprint of Dutton Signet, a division of
Penguin Books USA Inc. Previously published in a Dutton edition.
First Meridian Printing, October, 1993

First Meridian Printing (Revised Edition), 1997
1 3 5 7 9 10 8 6 4 2

Originally published in German under the title Abbruch der Schweigemauer.
"Ten Reasons Not to Hit Your Kids" reproduced by permission of Eppoch
and Jan Hunt

 REGISTERED TRADEMARK—MARCA REGISTRADA

LIBRARY OF CONGRESS CATALOGING-IN-PUBLICATION DATA

Miller, Alice.
[Abbruch der Schweigemauer. English]
Breaking down the wall of silence : the liberating experience of facing painful truth / Alice Miller ; translation by Simon Worrall ; with a new preface by the author.
p. cm.
Includes bibliographical references and index.
ISBN 0-452-01173-6
1. Adult child abuse victims. 2. Child abuse—Social aspects. I. Title.
[RC569.5.C555513 1997]
616.85'82239—dc20 93-34165
CIP

Printed in the United States of America
Original hardcover design by Steven N. Stathakis

Contents

Preface to the Revised Edition vii

Foreword 1

PART ONE
Openings and Glimpses

1. *Eve's Initiative* 13
2. *Out of the Prison of Confusion* 19
3. *The Psychiatrists' Campaign Against the Act of Remembering* 27
4. *Blindman's Buff and the Flight from Facts in Psychoanalysis* 41
5. *The Media and the Wall of Silence* 54

PART TWO
Facts

6. *Child Sacrifice as "Tradition"* 73
7. *The Monstrous Consequences of Denial* 78

   Adolf Hitler's Path to Genocide 78

   Nicolae Ceausescu's Vision of Redemption 94

8. *The Mistreated Child in the Lamentations of Jeremiah* 112

PART THREE
Giving Up Hypocrisy

9. *The Liberating Experience of Painful Truth* 129
10. *Protecting Life After Birth* 141

Afterword to the Paperback Edition 149

APPENDIX A *Wars and Dictators* 157

APPENDIX B *A Law Against the Business of Tyranny* 165

APPENDIX C *A Letter to Alice Miller* 170

APPENDIX D *Ten Reasons Not to Hit Your Kids* 172

Bibliography 177

Index 179

Preface to the Revised Edition

REREADING THIS BOOK AND CALLING TO MIND all the changes that have taken place in my own specific field over the last few years, my immediate impulse was to say no to a new edition. But my publisher, Arnold Dolin, usually the very epitome of tact and consideration, dug his heels in. That would be a foolhardy decision, he insisted; after all, the book was still attracting a wide readership. But this was precisely what gave me pause. The last thing I wanted was for readers coming new to the book to be confronted with a description of a situation that has since undergone a considerable degree of change. Most importantly, the problem of child abuse has finally received the attention that I had been so insistent in clamoring for. This is not, of course, to suggest that the fears and resistances that I describe in the book as specifically bound up with the subject of childhood have disappeared for good. But the sheer mass of material published on this topic has made it impossible to ignore or play down the facts of the matter any longer. Today no judge can behave as if there were no such thing as sexual abuse in the family and blithely grant an incestuous father visiting rights. It is also safe to assume that a great deal has changed in the way analysts, psychiatrists, and other therapists approach their work. Many colleagues have reported on their experiences with new therapy approaches that finally take adequate account of the importance of the life history written into their patients' bodies and face up to the crucial significance of emotional blockages.

I still get letters from people writing to say that it is this book of mine in particular that has given them the courage to fight against the pressures of their own immediate environment and to actively espouse truths that they had hitherto failed to take seriously, although they had intuitively sensed the justice of them. These letters demonstrate that the book still has a future; the positive developments in therapeutic care have by no means made the message it conveys superfluous. By arousing strong emotions, it provides food for thought and gives people the courage to act.

The title of the book is an accurate reflection of my feelings in 1989; it is admittedly less closely attuned to the present situation. When I wrote it, I really did feel as if I was fighting a lonely battle against a wall of silence, waging a hopeless war against the refusal to understand and acknowledge the crucial importance of childhood. Knowing that this refusal was the expression of unconscious anxieties rather than conscious decisions did not make things any easier. What, after all, can one do to combat another person's fears? One cannot argue them away or force people to embark on a course of therapy. Enforced therapy does no good to anyone. A person can change only himself, nobody else. Does that make the communication of knowledge a futile exercise?

I do not think so. My conviction is that sharing knowledge is necessary and that one must assist in the dissemination of vital insights as long as one has the opportunity of doing so. But there is always an element of chance involved; one never knows where the good seed will fall—whether on fruitful soil or on a patch of concrete by the wayside.

In the last few years it has become apparent that, given time, certain blind spots in public awareness will remedy themselves almost of their own accord. All it requires is for a few individuals in different places to encounter the same phenomenon, to face up to it, and to report unflinchingly what they have seen. Today, at all events, we can say that many of the taboos that I attempted to break with by writing as provocative a book as this one have since lost much of their power to harm. Both specialists and the media are now much more intrepid in exploring the subject of childhood. As far as public awareness is concerned, this has set in train a development that can no longer be halted, despite the massive setbacks we are encountering at present. These rapid changes call either for an adaptation of the text of this book to the new situation or at least for some reflections on that new situation, which I hope to supply with this Preface. It is in that spirit that I want to cite the following points:

1. The pugnacious style of the book has remained unchanged, although it no longer corresponds entirely to my present frame of mind.
2. My severe criticism of the experts would need to be toned down, as in this blanket form it is no longer a true reflection of present-day reality.
3. Certain statements (e.g., in connection with forgiveness and abortion) would have to be revised in the wake of the discussion and gratifying extension of my ideas by other authors. I share the opinion of Pete Walker (in *The Tao of Fully Feeling*, 1995) that the state of forgiveness cannot be a final one like the

feeling of love, which is sometimes bestowed upon us and sometimes evades us.

4. In the last few years I have come to the conclusion that primal therapy is not always free of dangers, that it is imperative for it to be embarked upon under expert guidance and not as a form of self-therapy. This conclusion is tantamount to a retraction of my earlier ideas on this subject.
5. Numerous studies on cult groups have enlightened us on the latest methods of human manipulation. It transpires that these groups frequently use primal-therapy techniques to brainwash the members they have recruited into a state of regression and thus make them completely docile and malleable. Thus primal therapy runs the risk of being misused for commercial purposes and reinforcing the individual's dependency on the group rather than encouraging his autonomy, as I had originally hoped. Today, however, therapists are using new approaches with awareness both of the advantages of primal therapy (its closeness to feelings) and of its dangers (manipulation and addictive-dependency on pain), and they attempt to use this awareness to the benefit of their patients.

I must ask for the reader's indulgence in keeping these points in mind while reading the basically unchanged text. Updating the text thoroughly would have too drastically altered the character of this book. Therefore I decided only to make some deletions, mostly of references to therapies that seemed to me effective seven years ago but that I would not want to recommend today.

In my preface to the paperback edition of Jean Jenson's *Reclaiming Your Life* (Meridian, 1996), I have set out my queries and doubts in connection with primal therapy; I would refer the reader to that text for a more extensive discussion of the subject. Shortly after the publication of the new version of *The Drama of the Gifted Child* by Basic Books in January 1994, letters from readers and subsequent research on my part made me realize that my recommendation of primal therapy as a form of self-help had been premature. The swift initial successes were unfortunately not of lasting duration, and many correspondents reported that the anguish aroused in the process was too great to be borne alone. So it became obvious to me that it is all but impossible to live through and dissipate these anxieties without expert guidance. At the same time, the awareness was borne in upon me that in a state of regression it is not possible to judge the competence and integrity of the person one has turned to for such guidance. This opens up all kinds of opportunities for abuse. The intensive phase with which primal therapy begins is an immediate obstacle to the formation of a balanced, critical, independent assessment of the therapist's abilities by the client. The fact that the attendant uncritical and irrational expectations of healing and "salvation" can lead to the establishment of totalitarian sects is borne out by the crass example of mass abuse at the hands of the exponents of "feeling therapy" as described in detail by Carol Lynn Mithers in her book *Therapy Gone Mad: The True Story of Hundreds of Patients and a Generation Betrayed* (1994). But this study was possible only after the community she describes had disbanded, something that frequently takes decades. Today we know that such groups exist and that members of sects are done irremediable harm before they become aware of the fact. And when their dilemma finally does dawn on them, it is frequently too late to do anything about it because they have lost all contact with their original social background and hence have no sources of moral support or financial assistance outside the sect, to which they are then frequently shackled by the debts they have run up.

Despite the eloquence of Mithers' example, I would still not have been fully alive to the danger of abuse inherent in primal therapy without the information on the way sects operate that I derived from the publications of the Swiss journalist Hugo Stamm, who interviewed me for a weekly magazine. The literature on cult groups helped me understand the psychological mechanisms exploited by sects and similar groups the world over. Gurus bent on maximizing their commercial gains and personal power profit to a high degree from the loss of the perceptive faculties forfeited by so many people early in childhood.

I am often asked why my books have an emotional tenor not usually encountered in psychological literature. I have been accustomed to responding to this question with references to spontaneous painting and my own pictures. This indeed is the gist of my remarks in the preface to the new edition of my watercolors, *Pictures of a Childhood* (Meridian, 1995). But strictly speaking, painting was preceded by another event in my life that provides a much more profound explanation of the way I write and the scientific interest I take in studying childhood. This was the birth of my daughter, who came into the world forty years ago with the congenital disability known as Down syndrome. My daughter's direct, spontaneous, and affectionate nature released me from many of the protective mechanisms I had developed, above all the fear that my love might be exploited. With her I had no need to protect myself. At last I could love, trust, and be tender without any apprehensions about my openness being misused for corrective educational purposes—as was the case with my mother—or my feelings being hurt. As I did not have the good fortune of enjoying an open and warmhearted relationship with my mother, this new opportunity for communication—for all its tragic aspects and the restrictions it brought with it—was more of a blessing than anything else. The spontaneity with which my daughter expressed her childlike, innocent, affectionate nature at whatever age she happened to be, and her sensitivity to insincerity and disingenuousness in whatever form, gave my life new dimensions and new objectives. My intellectual fixations stood revealed for what they were and in time were discarded. I countenanced only those things that were able to stand the scrutiny of my feelings. I became curious about my own childhood, a world that till then had been kept "frozen," as it were, in the confines of my intellect. It was this that prompted me to train for a career as a psychoanalyst and to start to paint. That was where the story of my childhood finally broke through. Today, I am convinced that I have only been willing and able to face up to my true feelings thanks to the existence of my daughter. She would tell me frankly and uninhibitedly what she saw in my pictures and what she felt about them, something that otherwise only very few people did. It was a kind of emotional communication which I found very precious, which took my own personal and professional development in a new direction, and is partly reflected in the style of my books, their emotional quality.

I have a great deal of respect for the way my daughter lives her life. It is something that in a certain sense I have learned a great deal from. Without the relationship with my daughter, I would have been even more remote from myself than I already was. Her dependency on me was a curb to my personal liberty but at the same time opened up avenues that brought me new discoveries. Thanks to this relationship, I have also found the courage to champion the cause of the child within us all, to fathom the consequences of infant dependency, and to respect the specific dignity of children. Their capacity for recognizing injustice even when they can do nothing about it is something that has opened up entirely new perspectives for me. In many ways it is only now, in retrospect, that I begin to appreciate something like the full extent of the boon that my daughter has been to me.

Among the restrictions that I mentioned earlier must be counted two wishes of mine that have not come true. The first was my intention to emigrate to America. In this I was motivated by the fact that I could communicate much more freely and directly there with people than I could in Europe. In America I have never felt that I was a "stranger," perhaps because so many people live there whose families come from other countries. The second is the creation of an institute that would file, catalogue, and evaluate all the "material" I have amassed over the years. I myself have only been able to respond to a fraction of the important letters, manuscripts, and books I have received in the last seventeen years on the subjects I have dealt with in my work and explore the implications that they represent. I would dearly have loved to pass on all this information to others for further research. But my life demanded of me a kind of organization in which to some extent the mother and the painter forced the researcher in me to take a backseat, albeit not entirely. However, as a researcher I had no one but myself and my inner life to turn to for support, no team of coworkers in an institutionalized setting. My consolation now is that my books have aroused a multitude of questions in the hearts and minds of my readers and contributed to ensuring that research into childhood continues to flourish. Today I rest assured in the knowledge that others—like Lloyd de Mause in the

United States or Elliott Barker in Canada and their associates all over the world—share the same concerns and will never allow a wave of ignorance to cast the world back into darkness.

—Alice Miller,
May 1996

Translated by Andrew Jenkins

Foreword

THE TRUTH ABOUT CHILDHOOD, AS MANY OF us have had to endure it, is inconceivable, scandalous, painful. Not uncommonly, it is monstrous. Invariably, it is repressed. To be confronted with this truth all at once and to try to integrate it into our consciousness, however ardently we may wish it, is clearly impossible. The capacity of the human organism to bear pain is, for our own protection, limited. All attempts to overstep this natural threshold by resolving repression in a violent manner will, as with every other form of violation, have negative and often dangerous consequences. The results of any traumatic experience, such as abuse, can only be resolved by experiencing, articulating, and judging every facet of the original experience within a process of careful therapeutic disclosure.

In recent decades, there have been a number of dangerous attempts to resolve the consequences of childhood traumas by violent means. Inevitably, they have all failed. Methods involving the use of LSD, hypnosis, or "rebirthing," to name but a few, have not only failed to lead to the integration of a person's individual truth.

They have, in many cases, resulted in even greater flight from the truth by way of new forms of defense such as addiction and other forms of denial, for example through political or religious ideologies.

Many young people who, driven by desperation and curiosity, have experimented with psychedelic drugs found themselves having experiences that were terrifying, discouraging, and totally misleading—experiences that would later bar the way to insightful and effective therapy. Often, they found themselves suddenly confronted by the full horrors of their childhood—without any kind of preparation—and were overwhelmed by symbolic images that rather obscured the reality. Not surprisingly, they would later do everything they could to avoid having to confront *these* experiences anew. What they didn't know is that what they had experienced and what was sometimes sold to them as "therapy" was in fact just its opposite: a traumatization that served to cement the confusions of childhood with symbolic contents, leaving in its wake a rigid sense of their histories that would later prove hard to resolve.

The consequences of such experiences are regrettable in the extreme. From then on, those involved placed their trust not in the truth, but in a chimera of addictions, specious theories, or medication. The possibility of facing the truth by means of a slow therapeutic procedure seemed inconceivable to them.

We build high walls to screen ourselves from painful facts because we have never learned whether or how we can live with this knowledge. "And why should we?" some people might say. "What's done is done. Why should we go over all that again?" The answer to that question is extremely complex. In this book, I will endeavor to show, by way of various examples, why the truth about our childhood is something we cannot, and should not, forgo, either as individuals or as a society.

One of the reasons is that behind the wall we erect to protect ourselves from the history of our childhood still stands the neglected child we once were, the child that was once abandoned and betrayed. It waits for us to summon the courage to hear its voice. It wants to be protected and understood, and it wants us to free it from its isolation, loneliness, and speechlessness. But this child who has waited so long for our attention not only has needs to be fulfilled. It also has a gift for us, a gift that we desperately need if we truly want to live, a gift that cannot be purchased and that the child in us alone can bestow. It is the gift of the truth, which can free us from the prison of destructive opinions and conventional lies. Ultimately, it is the gift of security, which our rediscovered integrity will give us. The child only waits for us to be ready to approach it, and then, together, we will tear down the walls.

Many people do not know this. They suffer from anguishing symptoms. They go to doctors who fend off the necessary knowledge just as they themselves do. They follow the advice that these doctors offer, subjecting themselves, for example, to completely unnecessary operations or other damaging treatments. Or they down sleeping pills to erase the dreams that could remind them of the child waiting behind the wall. But as long as we condemn it to silence, the child's only recourse is to express itself in another language—that of sleeplessness, depression, or physical symptoms. And against these reactions, drugs and tablets are of no help. They simply confuse the adult even more.

Many people are unaware of this, though some have long since sensed this truth and can nonetheless not help themselves. Some sense that to repress feelings of their childhood is to poison the very well-springs of life; they know that though repression may have been necessary for the child's survival—otherwise it might literally have died from the pain—maintaining repression in adult life inevitably has destructive consequences. But in the absence of any other alternative, they regard such consequences as a necessary evil. They don't know that it is indeed possible to resolve childhood repression safely and without danger, and learn to live with the truth. Not all at once. Not by recourse to violent interventions. But slowly, step by step, and with respect for their own system's defense mechanisms, recovery is possible.

I myself did not know this for many years, either. My training in and subsequent practice of psychoanalysis had made me blind to the possibility. But the success of my own experience of the slow integration of individual aspects of my childhood has made me want to pass on that information to all those who suffer because they are cut off from the roots of their own being.

Today we can be helped to correct our blindness, to resolve the consequences of old injuries, to access the truth and restore the crucial contact with the child in us so that we can regain those parts of our consciousness that were alienated from us for so long.

What is valid for the individual is also valid for the development of a wider social consciousness. Here, too, the monstrous truth regarding the causes and consequences of child abuse and the way that violence can be bred into human beings cannot be admitted to consciousness all at once, but must proceed slowly, step by step. To make this clear I would like to cite an example from my own work.

After the appearance of my first three books in the early 1980s, I was asked by a number of newspapers and magazines to contribute articles. But when I made it known that I intended to write about violence in the family, interest in working with me quickly evaporated. The only exception to this was the editor of the German magazine *Brigitte*, which, in 1982, went ahead with the publication of an article by me on the sexual abuse of children, despite the resistance of a number of the staff. The article bore the title "Daughters Are Breaking Their Silence" and was later incorporated into a revised edition of my book *Thou Shalt Not Be Aware*. It describes the courage of a group of American women in publicizing accounts of severe childhood injury so that they no longer had to be left alone with this terrible and destructive secret. They also wished to help other women to break down the wall of silence behind which society has sought to protect itself from the truth about cruelty and abuse in childhood. These women realized that the protection this wall appeared to offer in fact had destructive consequences for the survivors of child abuse. They also discovered that the number of people affected represented many more than they had imagined.

At that time, the subject of child sexual abuse was absolutely taboo in Germany; the effect of the article was like a dam burst. Hundreds of women, from all walks of life, wrote to the editorial staff and to me. They told of brutal childhood abuse. And they described the conspiracy of silence that barred them from these experiences and, thus, from acquaintance with a large part of their own personalities. Running through all these letters, like a refrain, was this sentence: "This is the first time I have ever spoken of this to anyone." Many of them added: "You may publish my story so that other women, who have experienced the same thing, may know that they are not alone. Until the appearance of your article I had thought that I was the only one to whom this had happened. But I must ask you, on no account to publish my name."

Most of these women were married and had children. Many of them had already been through "therapy." But neither with their husbands nor with their therapists had they dared mention their childhood traumas. In their entire environment, they found not a single enlightened witness, a person who could have at least partially freed them from their imprisoning secret, if by no other means than by simply heeding their suffering. As a result, the experience that had marked their entire lives and that returned to haunt and poison them in their fantasies had to be completely repressed for years. The image I had of each of these women at the time was of a little girl standing behind an immense wall, a wall in which not the smallest opening that could have held out a glimpse of hope to her in her loneliness could be found. Since then, much has changed. First, a self-help group called "Wild Water" (*Wildwasser*), which became the model for similar groups set up all over the country, was founded in Berlin. Not surprisingly, when it came to dealing with local authorities regarding funding, they still ran up against resistance, prejudice, and indifference. But in the last seven years the wall of silence has been breached—at least as far as the sexual abuse of girls is concerned.

Without the help of the women's movement, this rapid progress would have been almost unimaginable. Thanks, primarily, to the women's movement, both the scandalous practice of the courts and the isolation of the victims of abuse have been made public. That has resulted in the exposure of horrific facts that had previously been accepted as "normal." But even the women's movement could not entirely give up its blinkers—and it would have been naive to think it might have been otherwise.

To recognize and integrate something monstrous from our collective past as a society requires considerable time, just as it does on the individual level, in therapy. To rush the process may mean that the mechanisms of denial are further strengthened. We still need our illusions, our "crutches," as we confront a new and painful aspect of the truth on our journey toward a complete perception of the child's situation.

As a result, the women's movement clung to a number of illusions as it broached the subject of the sexual abuse of girls. Above all, its members needed to believe that mothers could not be party to this crime. Because I refused to lay responsibility for female child abuse solely at the doorstep of the men and insisted instead that *both* parents owed a debt of love and protection to the abused child—and that a caring mother would have prevented such abuses from occurring—it became clear to me that feminists found my books problematic (see Alice Miller, 1990a and 1990b).

But in the years since, the women's movement has also arrived at the point where it can begin to live without the illusion that only men commit acts of violence against children. One feminist sociologist sent me the results of her study of youths serving prison terms for attacking and raping women on the street. As it transpired, the rape and debasement of anonymous women had nothing to do with sexuality, although these men are referred to as "sex offenders." Rather, they were motivated by revenge for the helplessness and defenselessness that they themselves had once suffered—a reality they had subsequently completely repressed, and continued to repress, to the detriment of others. What became clear was that all these men had been sexually abused by their mothers in early childhood, by way of either direct sexual practices, the misuse of enemas, or both. Various perverse practices were used to keep the child in check without its having the slightest chance of defending itself.

Thirty years ago the use of enemas was still regarded as accepted medical practice. In truth, it was never anything but an act of violence against the child, intended to keep its bowel functions under adult control. To see this clearly and to be able to expose this form of destructive behavior required considerable openmindedness on the part of the sociologist concerned. That she did not have to protect the mothers in this case meant that she did not have to mask the truth in any way.

The last thing I wish to do, of course, is relativize these rapists' crimes by drawing attention to this aspect of their past. The criminal acting-out of repressed injuries can never be thought of as a compulsive necessity. Had these men been prepared to give up their repression, such acts would never have occurred. Sadly, they are not prepared to do so; and as soon as they themselves become fathers they are in a position to take revenge on their mothers with impunity—under their own roofs, on their wives and children, beyond the reach of the law.

Their deeds must be shown in their true light, just as those of their parents and grandparents and the millions of other child abusers in previous generations, who have produced the rapists of today. Their perverted mothers were also the products of this disastrous chain of events.

The crime of child mistreatment is probably as old as the world. So that it can no longer continue to be committed under the guise of misleading terms such as "tradition," "normality," or acting "for the child's own good," we have to, at least at the cognitive level, make available the *whole* truth. In the course of this book, I shall try to do that. By constantly circling around a particular theme and viewing it from different angles, I hope to create openings in the wall of silence, through which we can see unimpeded the realities behind it. Glimpses? What use is that? one might be tempted to ask. And, indeed, a glimpse cannot be a substitute for one's own therapeutic work. But it can perhaps communicate a sense of the possibilities beyond the wall and, more importantly, arouse a healthy curiosity for life.

My own personal breakthrough began with the free-associative painting I started to do in 1973. Without this experience I would hardly have had the courage to face my history and to integrate my feelings.

People whose only experience has been the wall of silence cling to the wall, seeing in it the solution to all their fears. But if they have once glimpsed an opening in it, they will not endure its illusory protection. The idea of ever again living as they once did, bereft of their new-won consciousness, becomes unimaginable as they realize that what they once held to be life was, in truth, no life at all. Part of their tragic fate was to have had to live for so long without that realization. Now they wish to save others from the same fate, as far as is possible. They wish to share their knowledge of the causes of their suffering and how it can be resolved. They want to let others know that life, every life, is far too precious to be ruined, squandered, or thrown away. And they want to say that it is worth feeling the old pain, never felt before, in order to be free of it—free for life.

PART ONE

Openings and Glimpses

1

Eve's Initiative

I WOULD LIKE TO BEGIN WITH THE STORY OF A woman in her mid-thirties who wrote to me and, without knowing it, became involved in the creation of this book, above all, of the chapter on the media. I did in fact receive her permission to use the contents of her letter, but choose to keep her anonymous. I shall call her Eve.

What I learned of Eve's story is similar, at least at the outset, to many stories that I hear almost every day: maltreatment and confusions in childhood combined with harshness, ignorance, and unconcern on the part of her parents, who regarded this as a god-fearing upbringing. Later: addiction, suicide attempts, two broken marriages, three aborted therapies, occasional short stays in clinics, renewed confusion as a result of medication and detoxification cures—in short, one long chain of misery. In the midst of all this came the birth of her own child, a new victim, as this woman could not be a mother until she had mothered the neglected, mistreated, and disregarded child that she herself had been. In the end, with the help of a deep-going therapy, she managed to save both her life and her own motherhood. Which is to say she managed to save her child's future.

In this respect, her story is different from many others I get to read. Eve succeeded in retrieving, step by step, over a long period of time, what had been repressed. The work she did on herself lasted for many years, and, as she has indicated to me in her letter, she continues to remain open to other aspects of her past, which she intends to make conscious and integrate. In fact, after the first few years of therapy, she was in a position to free herself from her addiction, dispel her blindness, and begin to care for herself and her child. She is determined to stop the destruction of both their lives, and this she can now manage. Her addiction was the price she paid for her illusions, the illusions without which she believed she could not live. Today, she can.

What hampered Eve in the early years of her therapy was her consistent refusal to believe that parents are indeed capable of routinely torturing their children, without anyone interceding, because of their ignorance of their *own* personal history. Her body, her dreams, and her feelings, though, went on reporting the true facts to her—once she had begun to admit the truth, and once she was prepared to take these testimonies seriously and stop denying them with her alcoholism.

Her amazement at the unexpected change that began to take place in her life inspired in her the wish to share the knowledge she had been granted in therapy with others. That she was not alone had become clearer and clearer to her. As she had at one time worked in journalism, Eve had the idea of making films for television that would portray the situation of the child using her own experiences as their point of departure. As she had become convinced of the broad applicability of what she had discovered about herself, she assumed that the editors she approached on the subject would share her interest. My own experience had made it clear to me that this is rarely the case, and Eve, in fact, underestimated the resistance—the repression—affecting everyone. Again and again in my contacts with decision-makers in the media, I had run up against the symptoms of this repression, even when my work was explicitly sought after (see Alice Miller, 1990b). Rather than take a risk, they prefer to forgo information that might be of life-and-death importance for coming generations. So in order not to have to call their own parents into question for a single moment, they cling to outdated, destructive opinions.

Eve, of course, had not reckoned with this. She had certainly seen, during her own therapy, the immense resistance she had put up at recognizing her own insights into her parents' destructive behavior. She would, she said, have gone to any lengths to avoid seeing and having to live with the unbelievable truth about her childhood. But the certainty—indeed, the actual experience—that with every bit of truth she had the courage to face and take into her consciousness her body became healthier and less bound to addiction led her almost to forget her own resistance. This in turn prompted her to imagine that others were equally open-minded. She wanted to be able to use her own story to let other people trapped in addiction know that there was another way, that they did not have to go on destroying themselves for the sake of their blindness, that knowledge doesn't kill, but liberates.

Eve's conversations with representatives of the media, however, rapidly divested her of her illusion. Fortunately, she was now in a position to correct such illusions with open eyes, whereas in her childhood she had not been able to do so and fell into addiction. She was no longer compelled to rely on people who strove against the truth. In the course of time, she would meet other people who confirmed her experiences. One of the things she often heard from the editorial staff she approached was that the subject of child abuse had already been "done" and, for that reason, should be left alone. Otherwise, there could be the danger of "overkill."

Eve thought she hadn't heard right. To an editor she wrote:

> *We're not talking about just another "subject," like the umpteenth Grand Slam tennis game or the latest Egyptian tombs, in which so much technical effort is invested these days. Why is it never mentioned that in ancient times, half of all babies born were handed over to wet nurses, that 50 percent of them didn't survive, and that, because of that, their nannies were known as "Angelmakers"? Why is it that research on the pharaohs is so much more important than information that from the earliest stages of our civilization, child murder was a fact of life and that we are still far from being free of the heritage? And why is it that you can only find such information in specialized research projects and not in the mass media? Why did politicians recently disqualify the idea of establishing a professional counselling bureau for sexually abused women as "megalomania"? Ultimately, what's at stake is our future, whether we can begin to understand the causes of human misery and overcome archaic ways of thinking. It's a question of combating ignorance, the kind of ignorance that destroyed my life for thirty years and continues to destroy other lives. And it's that which I wish to hinder. Can it really be that so many people are oblivious to this? When I know the truth, isn't it my duty to try to do something to halt that destruction? Is it possible to write*

> *this off as simply one of many "subjects"? Surely this affects the very roots of our existence. Isn't it just this ignorance that is leading us down the path to destruction? I want to show you that your unwillingness to take on this new knowledge is not just an insignificant omission. Whether taken consciously or unconsciously, it is a decision in support of the destruction of consciousness, ultimately of life itself.*

Others—people I call "enlightened witnesses," who work for the truth about childhood (see Alice Miller, 1990b, p. 167)—have doubtless had the same experience as Eve. But it didn't deter her. To help young people in their fight against addiction, she was even willing to give concrete insight into the realities involved by making public part of her story. The people she contacted in the media, however, feared that the truth would come across as "pathos." After all, went their argument, everyone has had it hard; self-pity and martyrdom don't help anyone. Reminded of the language used by her parents, Eve gave up on these editorial bureaus. Instead, she made contact with the English group Eppoch ("End Physical Punishment of Children"), an organization committed to the same goals as hers (see Appendix D). The organization campaigns for changes in the laws governing the mistreatment of children in order to raise public awareness of the criminal nature of such behavior. Eve also wrote to me suggesting the founding of such an action committee in Switzerland and Germany.

This book is my answer to her letter. I am convinced that Eve's committee and other efforts by her and like-minded people will continue, and despite the weight of ignorance facing them, they will continue their work of enlightenment. This book is also proof that such initiatives can inspire others to take up the subject and report what they know from their experience.

Though they owe their impulse to different occasions, the various sections of this book are closely linked. They all circle around a single theme, hinted at in the example I have just cited: that the courage to change comes as we make available to consciousness, and work through, our anger at what was, and remains, destructive of life.

The immediate occasion for chapter 5 was Eve's letter to me, in which she set down her outrage that leading German newspapers saw fit to label my exposure of the conspiracy of silence surrounding crimes against children as "pathos." Her fury at "the feeblemindedness of the press," as she called it, made me realize that I had to address this subject with recourse to the facts available to me to document my views. It became clear to me that as long as I did not react to the use of such terms as "pathos," simply because I can imagine why such terms might be used, I was not honoring my responsibilities as a writer. Of course, as a therapist, I can tolerate a person's indifference and defensiveness if I know that she or he was knocked about as a child and brought up not to feel or be aware. But as a member of a society, which may well be in the process of being destroyed by, among other things, such potentially destructive attitudes, I feel duty bound to respond. To make light of the human capacity for empathy in face of suffering may well discourage other victims of child abuse from raising their voices and telling us of their experiences. It reinforces the wall of silence, the wall that we must demolish as quickly as we can.

2

Out of the Prison of Confusion

I FIRST RAN UP AGAINST THE WALL OF SILENCE as a child. For days my mother would ignore me in order to demonstrate her total power over me and reduce me to subservience. She needed this power to disguise her own insecurities to others and to herself. She also wished to deny her responsibility toward the child that she had not wanted in the first place. The needs and questions of this little girl simply ricocheted off this wall. For her part, my mother felt no need to feel responsible for her sadism. As far as she was concerned, her behavior was justifiable punishment for my wrongdoing. She was, as they say, "teaching me a lesson."

For a child who for many years had no brothers or sisters and whose father, on the rare occasions that he was at home, never offered his protection, this long, unremitting silence was an agony. Even worse than the silence itself was the child's doomed but persistent attempt to discover its cause. As in Kafka's *Penal Colony*, the accused was in this case denied any clarification as to the nature of her offenses. This omission, however, contained a message: "If you don't even know why you have earned this punishment, then it is clear that you are quite without conscience. Look within. Search. Try. Then your conscience will tell you what guilt you have brought upon yourself. Only then can you try to excuse yourself. Then, if you are lucky, you may be forgiven. But that depends on the mood of the powers-that-be."

Did I know that I had begun my life in a totalitarian state? How could I have? I didn't even realize that I was being treated in a cruel and confusing way, something I would never have dreamed of suggesting. So rather than question my mother's behavior, I cast doubt on the rightness of my own feeling that I was being unjustly treated. As I had no point of comparison of her behavior with that of other mothers, and as she constantly portrayed herself as the embodiment of duty and self-sacrifice, I had no choice but to believe her. And, anyway, I *had* to believe her. To have realized the truth would have killed me. Therefore, it had to be my wickedness that was to blame when Mother didn't speak to me, when she refused to answer my questions and ignored my pleas for clarification, when she avoided the slightest eye contact with me and returned my love with coldness. If Mother hates me, reasoned the child, then I must be hateful.

The memory of the isolation of those times, the loneliness of that child as it desperately searched for explanations of the punishment that was being meted out to it, remained completely repressed in me for almost sixty years. As a result, I betrayed that little girl, who wanted above all to comprehend her mother's irrationality in order to finally be able to alter her fate by bringing her mother, the mother she needed, to speak. I had to betray her because there was no one to help me see the truth and live with it. There was no one to help me condemn cruelty. Instead, I continued the lonely search for my own guilt in the mazes of abstract thought, which didn't hurt so much as naked facts. It also held out to me the hope of an orientation that I had been denied. Because that little girl's feelings were so intense that they could have literally killed her, they were repressed before they could penetrate her consciousness. Only in recent years, with the help of therapy, which enabled me to lift the veil on this repression bit by bit, could I allow myself to experience the pain and desperation, the powerlessness and justified fury of that abused child. Only then did the dimensions of that crime against the child I once was become clear to me. Nothing that ever happened to me in later life, however terrible, can compare with it.

Though I would subsequently come up against the wall of silence, I was never a victim of it in the same way I was the victim of abuse. Later, I could sense it, judge it, condemn it. I could stop myself being confused by it. I could defend myself against unjustified accusations and find the help I needed. I was not condemned to blindness. I did often come up against people who had more or less barricaded themselves from inner life, people who were incapable of a dialogue of thought and feeling. And I learned that such people often sought to compensate for their insecurity by seeking power. Their one protection was to evade the facts and seek refuge in silence.

But when I look back over those encounters, none of them, however painful, irritating, or simply regrettable, was as threatening or destructive as my mother's silence at the time of my greatest dependence on her. As an adult I could choose to confront that silence with questions and facts. I could evaluate a person's behavior and responses. If necessary I could simply break off the relationship. I also had access to other people, people who did not punish me with their silence or take liberties with me. As a child, I had had none of these choices.

I couldn't say: "I'll find another mother, someone who talks to me and respects me, a woman who doesn't treat me like so much air but lets me know what she is going through—a woman who knows because she is living consciously." As a child I had no choice but to suffer my mother's vindictive silence, and, because I was blind to her dishonesty and thirst for power, assign the blame to myself. Later, I would try to compensate for the loss of my own truth with philosophical speculation about "the impenetrable nature of truth." Because the facts were so brutal and incomprehensible I was forced to deny them. The price for this flight from reality turned out to be high indeed. It meant the curtailment of my full consciousness and enthrallment to feelings of guilt.

Since discovering my own truth I know that a similar fate has befallen countless others even though they may not—or not yet—remember the facts. Some clearly can, as is evident from the proliferating reports of child abuse from all over the world. Their authors do occasionally receive positive responses from people who, though they themselves may not have dared till then to look back, having been dissuaded at every turn, now feel encouraged by such revelations to face the history of their own childhood. Frequently, however, they run up against a wall of almost unimaginable ignorance. This wall is especially impenetrable in intellectual circles, whose members have armed themselves with all kinds of theories against the return of the repressed and barricaded themselves behind them. All kinds of superannuated, though as yet unexposed, theories are stylized into intellectual systems and pedagogic models. And so long as students meekly and uncritically tolerate the eradication of the truth, these theories will continue to be taught at our universities.

Students who have sought to treat the subject of child abuse in their final papers have, I know, generally had discouraging experiences in their discussions with professors. Those they consulted usually changed the subject as fast as they could, were evasive, mocking, or simply embarrassed. As a rule they advised their students not to pursue the subject. Students who persist in expressing an interest in the subject have even had to reckon with chicanery. The extent to which they can withstand such maneuvers depends on their own emotional development.

In one manuscript, which has sadly waited for years for publication, Lloyd de Mause describes the tragic fate of a brilliant scientist whose pioneering work about childhood in the United States of America was so ridiculed by press and academia alike that he finally committed suicide. (See Glenn Davis, New York, 1976.) So distraught was he to see his insights rejected by the father-figure at the university, that he took his own life. Had he been able to call his own father into question he would have been able to see through the fears of those who rejected his work. But in the fifties, that was even more difficult than it is today.

Such chicanery reveals the destructive nature of repression in the life of an adult and in the activities of many intellectuals. Hard as it is to believe, in the entire world there is not one single faculty in which a degree is offered in the study of psychic injuries in childhood. Isn't this an extraordinary state of affairs, when one realizes that almost all of us are victims of the mistreatment, open or disguised, referred to euphemistically as "child rearing"? Every one of us, I am sure, could recount volumes if we ceased to tolerate the wall of silence in us and dared to feel.

All too many people have reason not to wish to be reminded of the harrowing experiences of childhood.

Fearing their parents' revenge if they were to admit the truth, they obstinately cling to the notion that there is no such thing as *the truth*—only versions of it. That there is indeed such a thing as the truth of *facts* doesn't seem to concern them. One sees: Such deception is possible if one fears the truth of facts, actively overlooks it, and has at one's disposal an arsenal of apparently credible theories to keep oneself pacified and deceived. That shouldn't, however, prevent others from seeing through the deception.

There are no limits to the intellectual ruses used to repress the truth. As both victim and perpetrator have a vested interest in denying it, without being aware of the price they are paying by doing so, one shouldn't be surprised if a hundred years from now a philosopher may "investigate the question" of whether Auschwitz and Hiroshima ever happened after all. Anyone who has experienced how the truth stored in our bodies can be located and evaluated with remarkable precision will, however, no longer be prepared to put up with evasions and excuses. Endowed with the experience of my own truth, I study the walls of silence surrounding us and describe them in my books. Many people breathe a sigh of relief. They, too, begin to look about them and ask, though timidly at first: Can I really trust my senses, my memories, and my body? You mean, I don't have to go on believing that white is black and black, white?

No longer to be compelled to betray one's own feelings and senses, no longer to allow oneself to be deflected from the truth of facts by ideologies of any kind, is already to lend a hand in the demolition of the inhuman, destructive wall of silence—the wall that we were forced to respect as children and which has again and again resulted in fascist behavior.

Fascism makes possible every kind of crime because one person, the dictator, arrogates to himself the right to destroy life without being accountable in any way. *He* decides what is worthy of life and destroys whatever does not conform to his definition. People who have only been exposed to the language of violence as children come to accept it as the lingua franca, regardless of whether they later become the victimized or victimizer. More and more young people, however, are turning away from destruction and committing themselves to life. They follow the truth of facts, not ideology. They warn of the dangers of subservience, brutal conformity, and the parade-ground ethos, before it is too late for all warnings. And they will be more sensitive to destructive cadences than many of our supposedly experienced politicians, who go on honoring the lies of their brutal upbringing because tradition holds that such an upbringing is both proper and necessary.

The demolition of the wall of silence, against which the theme of child abuse constantly runs up, marks only the beginning of a long overdue development. It creates the conditions that make it possible to free the truth from the prison of misleading opinions and well-established lies. But for the full unfolding of the truth and its deployment in the service of life, more is required than a merely statistical grasp of the facts. Some people may, for instance, say, "Yes, I was often spanked as a child," while remaining, emotionally, miles from the truth—because they cannot feel. They lack the consciousness, the emotional knowledge, of what it means, as small, defenseless children, to be beaten and shoved around by incensed adults. They say the word "spanked" but thereby identify with the mindless, destructive behavior of the adult who violates, abuses, and destroys the child without the slightest knowledge of or concern for what he is doing and what it may result in. Even Adolf Hitler never denied that he had been beaten. What he denied was that these beatings were painful. And by totally falsifying his feelings, he would become a mass murderer. That would never have occurred had he been capable of feeling, and weeping about, his situation and had he not repressed his justifiable hatred of those responsible for his distress but consciously experienced and comprehended it. Instead he perverted this hatred into ideology. The same holds for Stalin, Ceausescu, and all the other beaten and humiliated children who later turn into tyrants and criminals.

The return of the truth only begins to announce itself in the moment that we turn the tables and the word "spanked" condemns itself as heartless testimony to the disrespect and humiliation inflicted on the child. Only once we have become capable of empathizing with the feelings of the abused child we once were, and rejecting the mockery and cynicism of our adult selves, do we begin to open the gates to the truth. Only then can we also stop being a danger to others.

3

The Psychiatrists' Campaign Against the Act of Remembering

IN THE UNTOUCHED KEY, *I DISCUSS IN DETAIL* the tragic fate of Friedrich Nietzsche. Using Nietzsche's example again, I would like to show what can happen to a person when his whole system of defenses suddenly collapses like a house of cards. This happens quite frequently, as the knowledge of mistreatment experienced in childhood does not allow itself to be suppressed forever. Because the so-called specialists—the "professional helpers"—have been taught, not only in their own childhoods but in their training, to ignore this fact and the truth of child abuse, they are completely oblivious to the fact that what they spend their days dealing with in their practices is nothing other than the effect of the traumatizations experienced in childhood.

Nietzsche's tragedy was certainly not an isolated case. Who does not know of similar ones? A defenseless child that is tortured and at the same time forbidden to defend itself, to cry, to scream, to rage—to live? A child from whom only obedience and good behavior are expected? The only thing remaining to him, if he has the talent, is to develop a dazzling intellect. Life escapes him daily. Abstract thought offers a chance of survival. In the meantime, the body seeks to express its terrible distress in other ways than tears and screams. It produces an endless catalogue of symptoms, in the hope that someone will finally sit up and take notice and perhaps ask the questions: "What is causing you such distress? Why were you sick more than one hundred times in one school year?" But no one asks such questions. Instead, doctors continue to prescribe their drugs. Not one of them comes up with the idea that, perhaps, Friedrich's chronic throat infections are a way of compensating for the screams he is forbidden to scream. No one makes the connection between his persistent attacks of rheumatism and the almost intolerable muscular tension from which he suffers. How are his muscles supposed to relax, anyway—when the hope that he might one day be able to give voice to the fear and fury stored in his body slips farther away with every new day?

As a grown-up man, Nietzsche is unable to find a female companion. Not surprisingly, after the disastrous experiences of his childhood, he can trust no woman. Though repressed, these experiences tick away in his body and soul like time bombs. Writing helps him to survive, but it cannot be a substitute for life. It can also not help him to discover the truth. The powerful feelings stored in his neck, head, and muscles have been blocked since childhood. Consequently, they are not available to expression, feeling, or comprehension. The distress of the physically and psychically abused child he was can only find expression in the language of Nietzsche's philosophy. Hidden in the coded language of the books, unnoticed by Nietzsche himself or anybody else, and entirely divorced from his brilliant intellect, this soft, gentle voice—the voice of the child he once was—continues to speak. Finally, at the age of forty-five, the pain he has carried in him so long breaks through, flooding his intellect like a torrent of water after a sudden dam burst.

On a peaceful street in Turin, Italy, one January day in 1889, Nietzsche watches as a coachman brutally whips his horse. Nietzsche throws himself between them, throws his arms around the horse and, overcome by his rising anger and sadness, begins to weep uncontrollably. But the man who has spent his life denying and suppressing the feelings of the abused child in him cannot cope with the emotions that now course through him. For that, he would need help. At the same time, these emotions will no longer allow themselves to be repressed. The labyrinth of the intellect is flooded like an abandoned mine shaft. Amid the flood, there is only a vacuum. There is no one there to help Nietzsche understand his feelings and the sadness of the mistreated child whom he symbolically sought to save in the form of the horse. There is no bridge on which his intellect and his feelings can meet. As a result, Nietzsche loses his mind. He will live another eleven years, but only in a state of total dependence, first on his mother and then on his sister.

What happened next? Nothing. What would happen if Nietzsche were alive today? Again, nothing. Nothing, at least, that would help him. Like as not, his psychiatrist would prescribe a dose of the latest pharmaceutical wonder drug to ensure that the patient continued to swallow down his forty-five-year-old pain. Such doctors are well versed in the treatment of genius. Look at Hölderlin, van Gogh, or Edvard Munch. With them, too, medicine succeeded in annihilating the truth and the pain.

Were a psychologist brought in to treat Nietzsche, then the old game of vacuous words would start up again. An abundance of theories will be mustered to "explain" the illness: the collective unconscious, the oedipus complex, the castration complex, the sadistic newborn, archetypes, mandalas, and so on and on. All this, of course, imparted with absolute conviction and considerable vigor. The theories are there to stop the child trapped in the patient from starting to speak and tell its story. Should the patient begin to scream, out of protest and desperation at such nonsense, he will be summarily classified as psychotic—that is, incapable of submitting to something called "psychotherapy." Once he has been so classified, his goose is well and truly cooked. All that remains is medication.

That is standard practice these days, proudly labeled as "progressive" by psychiatrists. "In the old days," they insist, "we used to have to put the insane in straitjackets. To quiet them down, we used to have to beat them. But today peace comes in the form of a tiny, painless tablet. Isn't that a marvelous development?" Doctors are capable of "treating" a patient's confusion with so much medication and so many theories that he or she will no longer bother them. Screaming is bad for you, doctors say; what you need is peace and quiet. In truth, such doctors have to eliminate their patients' screams in order not to be reminded of their own pain, the pain they have so successfully managed to keep at bay with their theories. That's why they appear in white coats—to tame the fury of the beasts. These physicians make their victims feel small and helpless until the end of their lives: they ensure their patients have been robbed of the remainder of their feelings and blocked on their journey toward the truth forever.

Psychotherapists have also been encouraged in their suppression of the truth by Freud, Jung, Adler, and their numerous successors. Like all of us, these teachers had to suppress the memory of their childhoods. But unlike Nietzsche, they weren't content with intellectual games, with their own and their readers' confusion. They did more. They founded schools of thought that would confuse the therapists of the future. In these schools and institutions they offered their students theories purporting to be scientific and medical discoveries. The product of their failure—the abstruse theories that had helped them to deny the truth—was thus sold by these masters as an efficacious remedy that contained the truth.

Their heirs would lecture Nietzsche on the inherent wickedness of human nature and the need to keep it in check. Such ideas are needed in order to conceal from themselves and others the knowledge of how horrendous the early years of life are for most people and the fact that it is this horror that makes them ill and really bad.

Is it possible, one might ask, that Nietzsche, a person who became a professor of philosophy at the age of twenty-five and dared as no one before him to expose the hypocrisy of our culture, did not see through his helpers' power play? In fact, it is quite possible. Were he to live today, Nietzsche would probably dutifully swallow his pills, say "thank you very much," and look forward to being helped by—of all people—these learned gentlemen who are not only unable to help him face his own truth but, in fact, have a vested interest in his not being able to do so. As a result, they employ dangerous drugs to destroy the very thing that has the potential to heal him: namely, his memory.

It wouldn't be easy for him to realize what was going on. Why should he? After all, he desperately needs help, and they assure him that they can provide it. He thinks, "Well, they certainly seem to know what's wrong with me, and anyway, after thirty years' clinical experience, I suppose they ought to know better than anyone else. So it must be my resistance that is preventing me from hearing the good sense in their words. What I must do, then, is eliminate that resistance so that they can help me."

Many patients today think just like this. How can they know that for the doctors and psychiatrists, thirty or forty years' work in a clinic represents just as great a flight from the truth as Nietzsche's philosophy? Every day, these men and women use all the power at their disposal to prevent the slightest appearance of a childhood story. Nor is this campaign waged without violence. They didn't hesitate to use insulin or electroshock therapy, which destroys the patient's organism, so long as they erased their patients' stories. How, under these conditions, can they have discovered the roots of human suffering? Naturally, the keys that could unlock these things, the specific childhood histories of patients, were available to them in their clinics—if they only dared touch them. But they are more afraid of these keys than of the devil. With the devil, you can at least make a deal. He would doubtless have nothing against your use of electroshock treatment—but with your truth, you are alone. If you want to face it, suddenly no one is there. So psychiatrists have left the key untouched for thirty or forty years and chosen not to know how psychoses develop.

Despite this, doctors behave as though they know everything. After all, they know the "right" doses of the medicines they "must" prescribe—and this kind of knowledge impresses people. Very probably it would work with Nietzsche too if he were alive today. Their way of talking would be a familiar music to his ears: "You really should try to stop complaining all the time. . . . Try and forget. . . . It doesn't do you any good to get worked up and fly off the handle. . . . Anger is dangerous. It causes headaches. . . . You must try and control your behavior. . . . Everyone has had to live with injustice at some time or another. That's life. . . . Your parents were only doing the best they could, and if they fell short of that goal, well, that's only human. You have to forgive them. Only by forgiving them can you become well."

How could Nietzsche or anyone else realize that these opinions, which are still regarded as right all over the world, are not only demonstrably wrong and even dangerous, but that their very opposite can in fact be proved true? In order to be able to notice that, a person would first need to have had experience of his or her awakened feelings. Only then could this person begin to gain access to his or her childhood, with all its consequences: the pain, the insights, the sense of freedom, the consciousness, and, ultimately, the peace—the peace that results from real "pacification," via the satisfaction of needs. Such an experience would enable today's Nietzsche to throw the medication in the garbage and say:

> *Today I know that we cannot be free if we forget, relativize, or forgive the horrors and brutalities suffered in childhood. Quite the contrary. To forgive crimes has been preventing me from feeling and realizing what was actually done to me since my childhood. I want to fight against forgetting, against the wholesale slaughter of memory in our clinics. I want to release the memories blocked in me. I want to remember what I was forced to forget and know why I had to do so. I want to find out where I came from. I will no longer allow anyone to divert me from that search, to numb and confuse me with medicine or fool me with their theories. My illness helped me to hear the voice of the child I once was, the voice that I had tried to silence for so long. And now I want only to follow that voice, because it has taught me more than all the books I have ever read. I want to rediscover my life, the life I lost, and I will find it, if I can say often and*

clearly enough what they actually did to me and how *they did it. I want to open the doors to the past, instead of keeping them bolted shut, as you do and as you demand that your patients do. They think that it is only lack of time that stops you from listening to them. Only very few realize that you don't actually want to hear, because hearing makes you afraid. And it is this unconscious fear of your own deeply repressed personal history that prompts you to the madness of wanting to annihilate your patients' memories with electroshocks, so that the child in the patient—and in you—does not dare raise its voice.*

But patients have the right to decide for themselves how they should handle their own past. You don't have the right to rob them of their memories and their history. That is rape. They should not be sacrificed to maintain your *defenses. And they will cease to be sacrificed, as soon as they are prepared to confront reality and take a very close look at their so-called "helpers."*

You say you never heard of such things at university? More's the pity. Then now is even more the time to learn elsewhere, namely within yourselves.

The fictitious Nietzsche of today, like the original a brilliant, successful man, who from his childhood on suffered from depression, might add:

When I was a child I had no other choice but to let women preach at my expense. But today I am not so defenseless. My justifiable anger makes me strong and aware. I can now see through the lies because I have stopped forgiving, stopped praying or speculating, stopped laying the guilt on myself for what my persecutors did to me. I began to imagine specific situations and to question them. In my fantasy I visited the apartment where I grew up and my school. There I saw my family: how they really *treated me and not how they later said that they were. It was terrible, but it was true. At school I found the arrogant, ignorant teachers who beat us with relish, but who constantly spoke of their duty, their duty to educate bad children. Now that I know how these people really were, I don't need to go on accusing myself. I am on the way to abandoning my illusions. Step by step. I dare to look my doctors in the face, my "helpers," and see through the function of their lies.*

All this enables me to see love and honesty when I meet it, something I could never do before. Today, I don't think that all women are witches. It's true, it was my regrettable fate to be in the hands of witches, the women who tortured me in my childhood. But only when I felt the full terror of my situation, and didn't try to relativize it as I had used to, did I see that the whole world is not like my family. I learned that there are such people as loving parents and loved children—if only too rarely to feel very hopeful about the future of mankind.

Today, I believe that to mistreat children as I was mistreated—to punish them, to forbid them to weep, to speak, to defend themselves, to revolt against brutal treatment—is the greatest crime that there is. It is a crime to discipline children so much that they become blind, dumb, and lifeless and then, later, to deny the whole thing. No wonder such children would later as doctors rather subject others to electroshock treatment than confront the repressed misery of their past.

The mistreatment of children is the basest, meanest crime human beings can commit against their fellow human beings and against humanity in general, because it insidiously deforms the personalities of the generations to come. As soon as someone mentions it, it will be denied. "You don't mean to blame your parents, do you?" will be asked in threatening tones. "Of course I do, if they commit crimes," I would reply. Why should parents have carte blanche to commit whatever crimes they see fit? No one is forbidding them to get angry or have feelings. Of course, they can have those. But they are not allowed to take their feelings out on their children. Destructive actions, unlike feelings, should be explicitly and publicly forbidden.

If you, psychiatrists and psychologists, stopped trying to evade the reality of child abuse and its consequences in the form of psychic illnesses, if you had the courage to take up and use the keys that your patients present you with every day but that remain lying untouched in your clinics, then doors would fly open and you would awake to life. Then you would be in a position to help others to live. But your present state is dangerous because you go on endlessly destroying the human organism's self-regenerating functions. And you even do this with a clear conscience, unnoticed by anyone, saying it is your "duty." I will find people who know from their own experience how damaging it is to preach forgetfulness and forgiveness. Isn't that just what your patients have done their whole lives, and is that not why they have remained disordered?

Your theories contradict the reality I have discovered with the help of my feelings. But as you have learned not to feel, and don't wish to change, you are incapable of recognizing these contradictions. I can do without your theories, though. I am no longer a child whom you can continue to fool. I can feel like a child but think like an adult, and this combination of feeling and thinking enables me to bear my own truth, to live, speak out, and feel outrage and stop being the victim of the destructiveness of so-called experts. Instead of going on preaching to me, why don't you open your doors? Your fear is no excuse for your destructiveness. It doesn't relieve you of the responsibility that you took on when you entered this profession. Fear must be felt before it can be resolved. But it is wrong to act it out by inflicting damage on others.

If you are afraid to confront your parents in your imagination, to question them and feel your pain, then you should keep your theories and your philosophies strictly to yourselves. If you practice them on your patients, you will inevitably damage them. And neither ignorance nor fear can free you from your responsibilities. Others will take up the keys that you have left lying around uselessly, and, in full knowledge of your actions, confront you with what you have done. So isn't it high time that you learned?

If a fictional Nietzsche and other victims were today able to feel, think, and speak like this, they would not turn to drugs, suicide, perversions, or criminal acts. Because by confronting the truth of our childhood we can free ourselves from destructive and self-destructive patterns of behavior. But to be able to deal with painful truths we need the active support of people who know that what was previously regarded as a sin—criticism of our parents—is, in reality, our chance of becoming healthy. Whatever happens, our bodies can't be misled. The body respects only the truth of our feelings and thoughts and in the long term is only prepared to cooperate with them. Sadly, young people are constantly discouraged from being honest. They are threatened with what we like to call "morality"—first in the family, then in church, and, finally, in psychiatry.

The real Nietzsche wrote: "We all fear the truth." He also wrote, "Error is not blindness. Error is laziness. Every gain, every step we take toward recognition, depends on our courage." To me, blindness is the fear of facts—facts that may cause us anger. But it is precisely the experience and expression of justifiable anger that gives us the courage to go forward. Tragically, in the fifty-six years he lived, Nietzsche did not find one single person who might have encouraged him to do what he so deeply desired: to "bear the truth." Lonely and isolated, for Nietzsche fear conquered that desire. Today, one hundred years later, he might have more chance of finding an enlightened witness to help him take the decisive steps toward the truth. Even that is not certain. A Nietzsche of tomorrow might well succeed. But he would still need our support. We shouldn't let the injured go on languishing for years in loneliness, desperation, confusion or "spiritual eclipse" because of our ignorance, fear, and resistance to learn from facts.

After I had written this chapter, I received a letter from an American reader. She enclosed what she described as an "alarming" article from her local newspaper in Washington, D.C. I quote extracts here because it reflects a growing tendency that I have observed in many countries. It is also an excellent example of what I have tried to illustrate on the previous pages:

TRAUMAS SHOULD BE FORGOTTEN AND NOT CONSTANTLY REEXPERIENCED, CONCLUDES A STUDY OF HOLOCAUST SURVIVORS

Jewish people who survived the Holocaust and went on to adapt to life after the war as best they could were able to banish their dreams to the unconscious so successfully that they can even screen off the dreams they have today. So concludes a study carried out by Israeli researchers. The result suggested that current methods of treating post-traumatic stress syndrome—from which Vietnam veterans also suffer—can in fact serve to aggravate the disturbance rather than heal it.

. . . At the moment, it is customary to treat such stress-induced disturbances by obliging the patients to recall their traumas and reactivate the associated emotions, a practice roughly equivalent to the opening and closing of wounds.

The researcher Lavie, by contrast, believes that it would be better to seal the wounds with psychic scars and help those who suffer from post-traumatic stress syndrome to practice forgetfulness.

"We believe that in some cases repression may be the key to healing," said Lavie. "The idea that a patient should go on reliving the trauma is absurd and should be stopped. Patients should be treated in the here and now. Their attention should be diverted from the experiences they have been through. . . ."

The supporters of the idea of healing through forgetting obviously are not aware of the price society pays for this "health." It is a known fact that the men and women who helped Hitler commit mass murder did not need psychiatric help. They adapted excellently to conditions under the Third Reich and later effortlessly made the transition to postwar life. They could easily forget. They held down jobs, started families, mistreated their own children—all without the slightest twinge of guilt. These people didn't dream. And they never for a moment thought that they had done something terrible by carrying out their "duty." Hitler and those like him were, indeed, proud of their ability to forget their traumas.

But surely we don't want to again pay the price for forgetfulness. It is especially tragic that the destructive and misleading idea of healing by forgetting should be recommended to precisely those who were victims of the Holocaust.

It is not true that post-traumatic illness can be healed by forgetting, despite the fact that many people try to heal it in just this way. They do so at the expense of their own bodies or of other people—their children, patients, students, or the soldiers who have to die in the "holy wars" perpetrated because those who initiate them refuse to remember. Such destructiveness, however, can only function so long as children, patients, students, and soldiers permit it to function—that is, so long as they do not have the courage to look their mothers and fathers in the eye, question their views, and voice their doubts at the dangerous opinions passed down from generation to generation.

4

Blindman's Buff and the Flight from Facts in Psychoanalysis

EACH TIME I HAVE EXPOSED ONE OF OUR society's sacred cows, such as the world of pedagogy in *For Your Own Good* or psychoanalysis in *Thou Shalt Not Be Aware*, I have provoked much anger. This doesn't surprise me. To be made to feel that you had been (as either a child or a patient) duped for decades by people whom you loved and trusted, that in defense of their fear you had been abused and even sacrificed, is exceptionally painful. As a result, many chose not to confront the painful facts and go on ignoring the realities that I had uncovered. They went on defending their sacred cows. Indeed, the shakier were the foundations on which they rested, the more zealously they defended them.

At first, I didn't understand why my research and findings caused so much fear. Only later did the reason become clear. But as I felt myself to be quite definitely moving toward the truth I didn't let such evasive reactions unsettle me. I continued to search, until I arrived at where I stand today. And where I stand is clearly visible from my new books.

Some reactions to my work on the mistreatment of children have been reminiscent of the behavior of dogmatic religious groups. But it was not my goal to enter into a dialogue about articles of faith. I wanted to *disprove* established dogma with facts. Finally, I came to realize that this was actually a pointless undertaking as long as the other *does not wish to see* because he or she is too afraid of the facts. "We've all had our ears boxed because we drove our parents to distraction, haven't we? That's perfectly normal. How is a child meant to learn except by being taught a lesson, anyway? One shouldn't constantly dramatize perfectly harmless events and keep writing about them. I mean, without a few knocks along the way, none of us would be as successful as we are today."

That most people speak like this is a well-known fact. But I was amazed to hear such words from analysts when I raised the question of child abuse in conventional upbringing. They seemed truly not to know what I was talking about. I thought, if they spend eight hours per day listening to the victims of child abuse, then they must know more than people in other walks of life. At the time, I didn't have the courage to admit to myself what I actually already knew from experience: that is, how successfully and permanently these victims are prevented from finding, feeling, and telling their true stories. This holds, despite differences of vocabulary, for liberal as well as for conservative circles.

My former colleagues' evasive and fearful reactions are not personal—they arise because of the issue I advance. As I radically challenged Freud's theories by treating a subject that he wished to bury under the weight of taboo (see *Thou Shalt Not Be Aware*, p. 107ff), I clearly aroused many people's fears. Others had taken similar steps as I, albeit in less radical form, and they too had met with conspicuously similar reactions. When

Freud's favorite disciple, Sandor Ferenczi, dared to raise the subject of child abuse at a congress in the thirties, he was promptly dropped both by Freud and by his so-called "friends." Leading cadres of the Psychoanalytic Association like Ernest Jones and others even went so far as to continue to libel him after his death. He was bluntly called psychotic, although the famous British psychoanalyst Michael Balint could testify to the fact that he wasn't. As far as I know, however, Balint did nothing to rid the world of these infamous lies. A similar fate met the American analyst Robert Fliess, thirty to forty years later. He, too, made this forbidden and taboo theme the subject of a book (*Symbol, Dream and Psychosis*, New York, 1973). It is significant and deeply to be regretted that his book has to this day found no publisher in Germany.

The outlawing of the subject of child abuse in psychoanalytic circles has a long history, dating back to Freud's betrayal of the truth in 1897 (see *Thou Shalt Not Be Aware*, p. 107). Because Freud could not bring himself to confront the truth about his own childhood, he made his students suppress the truth about child abuse wherever it raised its head. The consequences were far-reaching. Several generations of followers, men and women, allowed themselves to be blinded to the truth as well. As a result, their patients seldom dared to question psychoanalysis's instrumentarium of power or its misleading interpretations. Thus, they failed to make their own the insight that psychoanalytic theory, be it Freudian or Marxist-Freudian, was ultimately a defense strategy: defense against the real contours of childhood pain.

Fear of the repressed realities of childhood is absolutely legitimate, of course, its causes plausible. But to try to master that fear at other people's expense is a dangerous practice. What can happen when a doctor doesn't stop at self-deception in his flight from pain, but deceives his patients, even founding dogmatic institutions in which further "helpers" are recruited to a faith advertised as scientific "truth," can be catastrophic.

The price of such strategies, aimed at the total denial of pain, are the depressions and other symptoms suffered by not only the founding fathers of such schools of thought but also by legions of their patients. Thousands of victims of child abuse have gone into therapy with Jungians, Adlerians, Freudians, or Reichians and found themselves listening to theories, sermons, or snippets of Oriental wisdom. And though they may have varied from analyst to analyst, depending on his particular bent and personal history, ultimately all were constructed for the same reason. Confusing and destructive interpretations are uncritically accepted. In the process, they allow themselves to be diverted from the traumas that they suffered in childhood. If patients do begin to notice something, they often allow themselves to be talked out of their tentative findings. All doubts are branded as acts of resistance against therapeutic healing; finally, patients learn to abandon expressing the slightest misgiving. Thus, the blindness that their masters acquired in childhood is further reinforced.

One case I came to hear of illustrates the processes involved with absolute clarity: A forty-year-old woman witnessed with her own eyes her husband sexually abuse their twelve-year-old daughter. Alarmed by the emotional consequences, she sends the child to the same analyst with whom she herself had been in therapy for the previous eight years. After the first session her daughter returns home distracted, saying, "I never want to see that woman again. She is terrifying, Mom. She said there was nothing wrong with fantasizing such things. Children often invent stories. But what I need to do is find out why I want to cause my dad problems."

Over the years I have heard numerous examples of comparable nonsense expressed by analysts. The words of my colleagues and teachers during my own training as a psychoanalyst also still ring in my ears. I choose to cite this example, though, because the child's reaction is so unequivocal. This twelve-year-old can still react adequately to a situation in which someone is trying to talk her out of her own perceptions and experiences. By contrast, her mother clearly lost the battle to uphold her own truth many years before. After eight years of therapy, she, just like her analyst, had become a product of what is effectively a refined method of pedagogy. Neither will very likely ever be allowed to see that the bottom line of psychoanalysis remains unchanged: "Whatever your parents did to you, you deserved. Our job is to show you your guilt."

The majority of patients are helpless in the face of such a message, a message that has been inculcated in childhood. That's why they go along with this game of blindman's buff for years, until they have become accomplices and supporters in the battle against the truth, a battle that began with Freud. Their teachers, masters, and "helpers," however, see in the dependency of their band of followers a sign that they are on the right track. Unfortunately, there are no other signs.

Since turning away from psychoanalysis and emphasizing the importance of our feelings for the therapeutic process, I have sometimes been supposed to sympathize with methods of treatment that I regard as dangerous because they are deeply manipulative. It is, of course, impossible to defend myself against all such incorrect pigeon-holing, particularly as I often only hear of it by chance. But because fear of the truth about child abuse is a leitmotif of nearly all forms of therapy known to me, I try, in my books, to show this by citing appropriate examples. At the same time I distance myself, with good reason, from all methods based on forgiveness and reconciliation (see chapter 9).

In order to gain firsthand insight into existing forms of therapy, I visited several centers in the United States of America. Among them was one that claimed to be able to heal autism with the help of a therapy method known as "holding" therapy. In this therapy the mother, with the encouragement of the therapist, would forcefully hug her child. The idea is that, though the child's reaction is initially defensive, contact can thus be established with him or her. Later, this should result in improvements in the child's ability to form relationships (see *Banished Knowledge*, p. 53). The "holding" therapy is meant to communicate to the child that the use of force in the present—and, by implication, in the past—is well-intentioned. Force, the therapy implies, is used for the child's own good, and the child will be rewarded and loved for its tolerance in letting it happen. He will come to believe that force contributes to his well-being and is, ultimately, beneficial. A more perfect deception and distortion of someone's perceptions is barely imaginable.

I spent a day observing what happened in the group. I also studied close-ups of the children on video. What became clearer and clearer as the day went on was that all these children had a serious history of suffering behind them. This, however, was never referred to throughout the entirety of this purportedly successful therapy. In my conversations with the therapists and mothers, I inquired about the life stories of individual children. The facts I came across confirmed my hunch. No one, however, was willing to take these facts seriously or allow them to alter their view of the situation. When I suggested that simply letting out anger could not, in the long run, resolve the effects of the children's traumatization, so long as the traumas themselves were ignored, I met with fear and defensiveness. In my view, what was happening here was that children were being encouraged to display their feelings while at the same time being prevented from experiencing and verbalizing the *specific feeling* connected with past traumatization. The reason for this, it became clear to me, was that their stories inspired fear in both doctors and mothers alike. These children were thus denied access to the primary cause of their distress. At the same time, they were being asked to suppress still further what they knew so that they would on no account lose the love that their mothers had finally shown them. The pedagogic nature of this therapy lies in the fact that the child's love, as well as its longing to be loved, its ability to adapt, and, above all, its remarkable achievements if it senses the slightest bit of hope of love, are manipulated and exploited. An autistic child doesn't have that hope. But hope will be aroused each day by the embraces the child receives in the "holding" therapy, and the child quickly shows what feats it is capable of. However, the complete blossoming of personality is not the same as receiving good grades at school. Such a child needs more than hope. It needs the certainty that its parents can bear to face its truth, that they will not evade it out of fear or try to manipulate it for their own ends. In the "holding" therapy a patient cannot attain this certainty.

My warnings about the manipulative and, in my view, extortionate aspects of this therapy were published in my book *Banished Knowledge*. Nevertheless, my clearly made warnings have been distorted into benevolent agreement. Unfortunately, such mistakes happen quite often because manipulative therapists are not aware of the fact that what they think is useful (for others!) could be wrong and dangerous. They don't question their manipulation at all. Thus, there are some schools and programs in the U.S. and Great Britain that advertise using my name, mixing my name and principles with other names and "therapies" that I could never have recommended, such as the Hoffman-Fischer Quadrinity Process or others. I gave my opinion of Milton Erickson's work ten years ago in *Thou Shalt Not Be Aware* (p. 34ff), apparently without having been understood.

I cannot, of course, take responsibility for any misleading information given without my knowledge, but I want to make it clear that descriptions of new methods are now available for everybody who seriously wants to work in a reality-facing program, without pedagogical aims.*

My own liberation only became possible once I had grasped the fact that fear of the truth and ignorance are not our inescapable fate. We choose them. In contrast to children, adults *have* the chance of dispensing with repression without being killed by the pain. We *can* decide to dispel our blindness and the intellectual defenses ingrained in us by our upbringing. Only when I knew with certainty, because I had experienced it in myself, that destructiveness and self-destructiveness can be resolved, did I stop using up valuable energy trying to understand those who had caused unnecessary pain. Only then did I have the courage to take a dispassionate look at their deeds and condemn them. I then realized that it is useless to try to understand a person who doesn't want to understand herself and that, indeed, this had been the thrust of my entire life: as a child, a woman, a psychoanalyst and, in some measure, as the author of my first three books.

Since I have begun to state, both in print and in my conversations with others, that the mistreatment of children is the greatest crime that one human being can

*See, for example, *Reclaiming Your Life* by Jean Jenson (Dutton, 1995; Meridian, 1996) and *Facing the Wolf* by Theresa Alexander (Dutton, 1996).

commit against another—causing psychological deformation in the next generation and, thanks to the suppression of the truth by its victims, including therapists, going largely unnoticed—I have frequently been accused of being hard-hearted and uncompromising. How, people often say, can parents be forbidden to feel anger? Unfortunately, what gets overlooked in such "arguments" is that there is a great difference between feelings, which kill no one, and actions, which can. Of course, parents must be able to feel and express their feelings. What they can on no account be permitted to do is beat their children with impunity, to hit them or humiliate them in other ways. Such behavior can be injurious to any growing organism, cause lifelong damage, and should be seen for what it is: a crime (I discuss this question in more detail in connection with the letters cited in chapter 5, p. 56ff).

Parents who *can* feel, who are conscious of their feelings and realize that uncontrolled anger, though it may be triggered by the child, usually has little to do with it, are less in danger of acting out their rage in the guise of pedagogy. I use the words "guilt" and "victim," rather than "causes" and "effects," as I am often politely urged to do, advisedly. Children are turned into victims *by people*, by their parents, not by some kind of automaton. These people have no right to behave as though they were merely destructive automatons and adhere to their ignorance, even though conventional wisdom and even moral and religious teachings confirm them in their actions by preaching forgiveness to their victims. One day the effects of such opinions will be seen in all their destructiveness.

Sandor Ferenczi, Robert Fliess, and Heinz Kohut all endeavored to find out the truth about child abuse. They did not succeed because they remained analysts. They remained until their deaths in the dark labyrinth of analytic theory. In vain they waited for their colleagues to confirm their findings on the consequences of repressing childhood trauma, consequences that they discovered in patients' histories. Because they lacked the experience of their own childhoods, they allowed rejection by their peers to divert them from their goal. Had they found their way back to their own childhoods, they would not have needed this confirmation from outside. To live with one's own truth is to be at home with oneself. That is the opposite of isolation. We only need confirmation when we are alienated from ourselves and in flight from the truth. All the friends and devoted admirers in the world cannot make up for that loss.

Since feeling the almost unfathomable isolation of my childhood, I myself no longer feel isolated. This experience allowed me to free myself of redundant opinions and lay aside the blinkers that had become unbearable to me and that prevented me from fully living. As a child they were crucial to my survival. Had I seen and felt as a child how my parents mistreated me and what consequences that had, as I have today in its true dimensions, I would probably have died. As an adult I can live with that truth.

The life of Friedrich Nietzsche tells us much about the powerlessness of a brilliant intellect, bent on using everything in his might to stop the knowledge of the first, searing experiences of his life from welling up into consciousness. Nietzsche created grandiose works in which he struggles against the simple truth of the cruelly abused, and duped child that he had once been. Even as a school child he suffered from chronic rheumatism, headaches, and sore throats, without anyone's understanding these distress signals. In order to avoid experiencing, at any cost, what he had been forced to endure as a child (because no one would have supported him), he lost his mind at the age of forty-five.

Medicine has, of course, convenient labels for such self-destruction. But Nietzsche's breakdown in Turin was not something inevitable. It was not desperate necessity. It did not have to happen. And it *would not* have happened if there had been someone, one single enlightened witness, who could have helped Nietzsche bear the truth of his childhood and take his childhood sufferings seriously. But in the entire course of his life he never found such a person. For that reason, his life reached the tragic end it did—the end of a person who both searched for the truth and feared it like the plague. For it wasn't the truth that killed Nietzsche. Condemned to boundless loneliness, supported by no one, he capitulated to *fear of the truth.* One person, with enough courage to face the truth of childhood, could have pulled him back from the brink.

It is hard enough to recognize lies for what they are if only one person, one from whom we anticipate help, insists on maintaining the lie. Inbred tact and our own distress hamper us in contradicting that person. How much more difficult is it, then, to see through lies when everyone around us takes them for the truth, simply because they themselves are victims of such lies. Thus, yesterday's victims become the opinion-makers and power-brokers of tomorrow.

In 1989, the French magazine *Paris Match* published the results of a poll in which 78 percent of the high-school students questioned stated that the beatings they had received as children were necessary and just. This confirmed my view that, contrary to the belief of many of my critics, public support for corporal punishment and other forms of physical abuse is not a thing of the past. Moreover, this study showed with horrifying clarity how lies inculcated in youth become adult opinions and convictions. As such views are held by the majority, they are for many people all the more difficult to see through, especially when correct information is lacking. Adolescents who have been beaten regard what they have experienced in their own upbringing as normal and as a matter of course. They think that what they have been taught—namely, that children need to be beaten—is right. And they don't question these views, because as children who have been physically intimidated, they are afraid to call their parents into question. As a result, they adopt the destructive and ignorant views of their elders. They *don't know* that there *are* people who love their children and would never use violence against them, and that such children do not grow up to be criminals or tyrants but happier, more conscious human beings who help others and would never wish to harm them. That is also true of people who, though they were damaged in childhood, have been able to resolve the blinding results of these injuries and can, therefore, categorically condemn such destructive behavior toward children.

This knowledge is so crucial to the survival of this planet that one would think that the newspapers would wish to inform the reading public of it daily, in order to warn people against such dangerous, false prophets. Why aren't the church bells rung to warn the faithful against relinquishing their democratic rights and putting themselves in the hands of future tyrants—tyrants who reveal their true intentions unmistakably by their proclaiming of violence in raising children? We are now in a position to know and to test our knowledge in every case. Anyone who claims that the torture to which they were subjected in childhood was a "good upbringing" should under no circumstances be allowed to gain power over others, let alone over entire peoples. As we have seen, such people can easily become destructive leaders.

To sign away our democratic rights to future

tyrants and dictators, because they cast themselves in the role of "strong fathers," thus reminding us of our own, is tantamount to committing collective suicide. Even if we have, since childhood, been waiting for the great, redeeming figure who will solve all our problems (see chapter 7), as adults we can be aware that such a redeemer will, in reality, turn out to be something quite different. For it is more than likely that people who completely repress and falsify the mistreatment they once received will be a danger to others, a danger that increases the greater power they hold. This can be clearly illustrated by the lives of Hitler, Stalin, and countless of their followers. Among them will not be found a single person who became a tormentor of others who did not approve of the abuse he himself once received.

5

The Media and the Wall of Silence

THE CONFUSION AND FEAR THAT HAS ITS roots in the pain of one's own childhood runs through our whole society. At every attempt to share the new discoveries I made with the public, I, like Eve, ran up against the most determined resistance on the part of the media. It is true that I can go on publishing these discoveries in my books, because my publishers are already aware of the growing interest in this topic. But there are other people who have important things to say, and they are dependent on the press. They and their readers rely on essential information not being torpedoed. All too often, however, the media buttress the wall of silence against which all those who have begun to confront their own childhood rebound. Despite that, in recent years the wall has begun to show a few cracks and cavities, which are of great significance for us. This slow crumbling has been due to the efforts and courage of all those people who have decided to enter into a deep-going, reality-based therapy and have shared the insights they have gained with others.

In recent years I have not only spoken out in my

books, but, when it appeared to me necessary, reacted to distortions of the truth in the media. I would here like to make these reactions available to my readers, so that they can see they are not alone in their experience. Certainly, it is hard to share discoveries that were made in tears with those who regard their rigidity and emotional poverty as the only possible way of life. But those who no longer can nor wish to bear the rigidity they have maintained up to now are grateful for whatever information they can glean from people who have decided to make the journey into the buried, untouched, but profoundly influential domain of childhood. Such reports confirm the fact that their tears and their pain are milestones on their own journeys toward the truth.

Apart from the wish to support those seeking the truth, I wish to show that understanding the origins of one's aversion to the truth should not prevent us from impugning and condemning the destructive consequences of this stance wherever and whenever we encounter it. At the time of writing *The Drama of the Gifted Child* I had not as yet seen this so clearly. Thus, I received universal praise for my understanding and forgiving attitude. It is not enough, as I once thought, to simply reveal the facts. To change things, to stop the barbarous mistreatment of children sanctioned by a tradition thousands of years old requires more. The dismay and shock I had anticipated as a result of the revelations I made simply did not happen with many people, because they are fundamentally committed to evading their feelings and are skeptical about everything that runs counter to that attitude. As long as people like doctors, therapists, and members of the media—people invested with great responsibility for others—continue to deny or minimize barbarism toward children, we must reveal how and to what extent they do so. Both must be condemned. I regard this as part of my attempt to enlighten people on the subject of the mistreatment of children.

Instead of philosophizing in the abstract about "social structures," I draw my evidence from the facts of daily life. Anyone who does not go in fear of such facts can check and verify them. Those who wish to avoid these facts at all costs quite often go on the offensive. That, too, needs to be unmasked—so that such attacks cannot continue to injure or silence others and destroy the work they are trying to do on themselves.

The suppression of the truth about the crimes committed against children is a crime for the simple reason that it attempts to prevent us from saving both our children and our future. What is sometimes called by others the "impatient tone" of my latest books comes from my well-considered and completely conscious decision to withdraw both my empathy and my tolerance from those who not only, out of fear, remain indifferent but also actively participate in minimizing, veiling, and concealing the worst crime against mankind there is, thereby helping to ensure its continuation.

After a review of my last two books appeared in a newspaper, a review that sought to minimize the preventive measures that I regard as absolutely essential, I wrote the following letter, which I quote here in abbreviated form, to the editor:

> *You are living in a country in which two-thirds of the parents interviewed by the magazine* Eltern (Parents) *regard the physical punishment of children as necessary and correct. What this means is that millions of children are endangered, because their parents have not been taught to regard such behavior as dangerous. You surely know that despite the frequent coverage of child abuse in the newspapers, very few specialist studies are devoted to the subject. If they*

are, they are invariably read by a minority, because this subject is generally one to be avoided. Now, however, Banished Knowledge *has appeared, a book which, despite the general aversion to the subject, has been widely distributed and read. The author describes in this book the harm that parents blindly inflict on their children, why they do so, where it leads, and how this tragic situation can be avoided. Countless readers' letters show that this information is of use to them. The book gives you a chance to communicate such information to your readers. But what do you do with it?*

You allow a review of this book to be published in which it is suggested that a previously sensitive psychoanalyst has evidently lost not only her mind but her sense of responsibility as well. She has, according to your review, become a strident advocate of hatred, a fool who rushes in where angels fear to tread, someone who has allowed the mistreatment she suffered in her own childhood to blind her, making her see horrors where none exist. You have implied that she feels persecuted by blood-curdling fantasies.

It is hard to imagine a more thorough deformation of the truth. In fact, what I decided was to deliberately reexperience what it must be like to be the child of ignorant parents *and report my findings. I do so again and again to bring the sufferings of children to the attention of parents and society at large, so that grown-up attitudes and behavior can change. That* you *have decided not to support my efforts, thereby denying your readership important information, is deeply regrettable for socio-political reasons.*

Nine years ago, my book The Drama of the Gifted Child *was heaped with praise by your newspaper because it implied that child abuse was an unresolvable tragedy. In that sense, it obliged no one to do anything about it. Now that I have shown that such a tragedy can indeed by averted, the conclusions of my books are promptly suppressed. But isn't the subject as old as the hills, and therefore not worth covering? Sadly, it isn't. Otherwise, the world would be a different place. And we no longer have time to lose before we open our eyes to these new discoveries. Are you really determined to see that the number of parents who mistreat their children is on no account diminished in Germany? I can hardly believe so. But having read the review published in your newspaper, I have no choice but to ask myself that question.*

After the reviewer had apologized for his "unintentional" libel, I wrote the following letter, which the newspaper subsequently published:

The editing of a passage cited in a review of my books The Untouched Key *and* Banished Knowledge *has led to a confusion of the issues. The relevant passage of* Banished Knowledge *(p. 155ff) reads:*

"Repressed, unconscious hatred has a destructive effect. Hate that we have experienced *is not a poison, but one way out of the trap of distortion, hypocrisy, or open destructiveness."*

Taken in context, what I meant was that the conscious experience of hatred in therapy protects us from blindly living out and displaying our hatred. What is involved here is the crucial distinction between experiencing *a feeling and* acting it out *in ways which, under certain circumstances, can destroy human life. This distinction is one of the fundamentals of my work, without which it can hardly be understood. By omitting the italics in the phrase "hate that we have experienced" (as opposed to hate that has been repressed), by ignoring the context (that is, the therapy), and by using the misleading word "praises," you suggest that the author is irresponsibly counseling her readers to act out their hatred. Such an implication misrepresents everything that I have ever written or advocated. On numerous occasions, in fact, I have warned of the dangers of precisely that course of action with reference to the example of Adolf Hitler. I do not "praise" hatred, and I do not encourage people to act it out against their parents. In* The Untouched Key, *I use the example of Abraham and Isaac to show quite clearly that this is indeed no way to solve anything, and that there are humane and effective ways of freeing ourselves.*

At the end of 1989 a respected weekly newspaper decided to publish what passed for a review of my new books in which it was held that I had already said everything there was to say about "the poor children" in *The Drama*. In their view, the subject was a closed case. All my subsequent books were, therefore, an unnecessary repetition of the same old song, something that was probably to be expected of me in the future.

I attempted to bring to the situation of the newspaper's editor the fact that not a single word had been written to validate this "opinion" and that the content of my new books had been utterly suppressed. Such a course of action seemed to be routine for the editors concerned. No one showed the slightest surprise. The letter cited here, which the newspaper published with the omission of the last sentence, describes the details:

The title of the review—"Established Knowledge"—makes a claim that its content refutes. If it were really the case that knowledge of the origins and consequences of child abuse (the subject of my last two books) were a well-established fact in Germany, if this knowledge were indeed not still banished—then your reviewer would not be able to make light of the subject in public. The fact that he has proves just the opposite.

The impression given by the article is one of someone keeping his ears tightly shut, so that he does not have to hear something that he does not wish to hear. Evidently the person concerned took more than a year to so much as read the dust-jacket of my book. Clearly, however, he only managed to get halfway through the first sentence, which reads, "As in her previous books, Alice Miller is here concerned primarily with facts." *Even this sentence evidently sent your reviewer into a psychological tail-spin. He writes: "Alice Miller's concern is here, as it was before—indeed, what* is *her concern? The informed reader doesn't even need to open this book." And the confused reviewer doesn't even need to read the books under review. This decision apparently simplifies his existence.*

Above all, I find it shocking and regrettable that the theme of child abuse, and its victims, can be treated with so much scorn by your newspaper. This disregard of human suffering evokes memories of the darkest time in your history.

One man's valuable information, one could say, is another man's poison. People who wish to resolve their repression discover valuable information in my books. Certain reviewers, duty-bound to read these books, are, by contrast, clearly out of their depth. They find themselves suddenly—and wholly unprepared—face to face with the sufferings of their own childhood, without any useful weapon at hand to fight off the old confusion and perplexity. Thus, they ensure in advance that such books have nothing to say to them, taking refuge in well-dug-in intellectual foxholes. On one of many such occasions, it seemed to me worth reacting, and so I wrote the following to the reviewer:

> *1. It is not one of my theories, but a fact, that the mistreatment of children leads to destruction and self-destruction, and thereby to suffering in the world. If you can find valid arguments that contradict this claim, I would be grateful. Until now I have heard of none that can.*
>
> *2. Beyond that, it is not simply* my *problem if the experts do not see this danger. On the contrary, it is more their problem, because they lay themselves open to attack and deliver proof of their blindness. Doubtless, they will go on seeking refuge in the bunkers of their unworkable notions long after other people have already begun the unpleasant task of confronting the facts, so as to do something about the wretched state of the world. Thanks to that confrontation, other, less closed-minded, experts will recognize the theoretical deceptions of "authorities" like Freud for no less than what they are: namely, strategies to ward off fear of one's own childhood history.*

In contrast to the intellectual distance and vagueness of the last example, another review ended with a catalogue of barely concealed slander. I responded to it only because of the way that it confused action and feeling, a misunderstanding that I have widely observed. I wrote:

> *In your review of my book* Banished Knowledge, *you correctly quote the following sentence: "If it were forbidden by law to take out anger against one's parents on one's own children, one would be forced to find other ways out of the trap and would probably find*

them." To which, you respond: "As if anger could be forbidden by law." From this extraordinary remark it is clear that you make no distinction between feelings *and* actions*—that is, between the feeling of anger and working out, or abreacting, this feeling on innocent substitutes (children). This distinction is, however, as crucial as the one between a good therapy and mistreatment of a child, or, put another way, between Kafka's* Penal Colony *and Hitler's gas chambers.*

As an absolutely central confusion is involved here, I would like to take the chance of saying something about it. Of course, one cannot and should not forbid anyone their feelings. However, the acting out of anger is not a feeling but a deed. *If it is directed against other grown-ups, it must not necessarily be forbidden—except in the case of bodily harm—because adults who are thus attacked have a* de facto *ability to see through such a misuse of their person and to defend themselves against arrogance by invoking their rights. Working out our rage on defenseless, dependent children, by contrast, can and must be forbidden because it is a crime that brings with it life-long consequences. A legal ban on physical abuse may already be imminent but psychic mistreatment continues to be practiced, and uncritically tolerated, under the guise of "child rearing." That individual journalists and certain supposedly progressive institutions shrink from publicly backing such a law merely increases the danger—in many cases, the mortal danger—to which countless children are exposed daily.*

In reaction to an article that dismissed the theme of "Hitler's childhood" as totally irrelevant, I wrote the following letter:

Thousands of historians have pored over the question, and will doubtless continue to pore over it, as to how Adolf Hitler could become chancellor of Germany during the Weimar Republic. You are correct in saying that Niklas Radström did not analyze this question in his play, Hitler's Childhood. *Instead, what he did was something that, as far as I know, no other artist has dared up to now: He placed himself consciously, and committedly, on the side of a severely mistreated child in order to see what happens when our adult society is placed under the microscope from that perspective. Much, indeed, happens. Even though he used my research to support his own work, he would never have been able to write such a powerful drama had he not been able to empathize with the child as much as he did.*

Sadly, it has to be admitted: working on our childhood frightens us. Certainly, it is not everyone's cup of tea and we are usually content to let others do this emotional and spiritual work for us. A knowledge of our childhood, however, is indispensable if we wish to really understand adult life. I regard the fact that Radström was willing to take this decisive step toward reality, consciously dispensing with unusable theories, as an event with implications that reach beyond the history of theater. The dramatization of the child's perspective, as enacted in this play, can contribute to a deepening of our knowledge and thinking. And not only in a political sense. The title of Radström's play was and is Hitler's Childhood, *and he was at pains to make it clear that what was meant was this one, single childhood. But he and I would like to distance ourselves from the phrase "for example" that was later added to the play's title. This arose as a result of very specific considerations on the part of the actors at the Zurich theater. I can appreciate such considerations, though I do not share them. The Zurich ensemble's decision is reflected in the* mis en scene, *which unlike that of the original Swedish production, did not portray Hitler's childhood, which, in its hideousness, seemed almost incredible, but chose instead to portray it as one that was simply seriously flawed.*

Had Hitler experienced even a glimmer of friendliness and kindness on the part of his parents—as was suggested in the Zurich production of the play—he would never have become the greatest criminal in the history of the world. He would have had the chance to register not only brutality in those around him, but other things, such as empathy for his fellow human beings. He never had this experience. The inflexibility of his attitude, an attitude that knew neither pity nor exceptions in its destructive fury and that found perfect expression in the monstrousness of the "Final Solution" and the euthanasia legislation passed by his regime, all bear witness to that fact. His psyche registered only hatred, violence, and pitilessness. This total, unqualified experience—the experience of a child growing up with its own parents—registered at a very early age, made of him what he would later ultimately become: the absolute incarnation of evil.

That letter was written in 1986. At the time, I knew of no other attempt to portray society through the eyes of a child with this degree of involvement and commitment. Since then I have read Manfred Bieler's book *Quiet as Night: The Memoirs of a Child*, published in 1989. I believe the appearance of this book is of great significance. Certainly, I know of nothing similar. What Radström attempted to portray by empathizing with another person's fate, Bieler re-creates from the reality of his own childhood suffering. In the book he takes the child he once was by the hand and leads it back through the forgotten horrors of its childhood. He shakes off the conventions of the adult world, which rob the child of its right to its own feelings and perceptions by making light of them. Thereby, he becomes its enlightened witness. He is able to do this thanks to a grandmother who sometimes protected him from his parents and by doing so was his helping witness. On one occasion, as the young Manfred Bieler was being mistreated, she even turned on the father. By doing so, she showed the child that an injustice was being committed against him. She also showed him that his father's actions were condemned by another grown-up, that the child was not entirely without rights and could live in hope of help. Many abused children have never had this experience. They therefore have no idea that they would not only have gotten help, but would have deserved it—if only someone in their environment had been a little less heartless, a little less ignorant. Bieler's grandmother also demonstrated with her affection that he was worthy of love. All this made it possible for Manfred Bieler to confront the pain of his childhood, not to totally deny it, and write about it. People who have had no helping witness in their childhood cannot do so. They need an enlightened witness in therapy, someone who could make access to the story of their childhood easier. Unfortunately, many "therapies" achieve precisely the opposite effect. They forever silence the child's story.

Some of the reactions to Bieler's book reflect the cynicism with which the emotional annihilation of children is often met. Critics, who regard themselves as "authorities" on the subject, treat this book with the same mocking tone as parents have traditionally greeted a child's words. Had these critics been capable of remembering with any vividness that such things may have happened to them as children, they might have had the necessary sensitivity to empathize with the plight of other children. By denying, making light of, or minimizing that plight, they are also totally denying their own feelings. And this is a habit they on no account wish to give up.

We will without doubt still need a lot of time before we can develop the necessary sensibility to enable us to recognize tendencies that are inimical to and destructive of life. But without this sensibility we will go on being the victims of blind and destructive actions, whose dangers we easily underestimate, because they impress us in a superficial way as intellectual acumen. In truth, they merely disguise destructiveness.

We must fight against the suppression of the truth in all its forms so that those who were themselves once mistreated, and regarded the suppression of the truth as normal, can see it for what it really is—suppression. Otherwise they will allow themselves to go on believing that *everything* they read in the newspapers is true.

The fear and defensiveness that many reviews of my books reveal is understandable, as they touch off people's own, repressed experience. Were there a willingness to resolve them, the memories that surface in the process of reading could be helpful. Unfortunately, it seems that even at the mention of the word "childhood," fear outweighs this willingness. Such is the negative gravity of defensiveness.

Not that this fear is consciously experienced. Rather, it is simply warded off by all available means. Some people seek to invalidate the subject of child abuse by insisting that it is merely my own personal problem, a problem, they say, that makes me see cruelty at every turn. Others claim, just as brazenly, that the subject is already "common knowledge." Still others seek to invalidate my findings as unscientific. They are "too simple" and "convincing," something, it seems, that is out of the ordinary and therefore arouses fear. One respected reviewer even went so far as to write: "What is problematic about Alice Miller's claims is that they are so damnably logical. In her last two books, she sets forth her theories with such cogency and persuasiveness that the reader, without even realizing it, is simply drawn along with her." This passage graphically illustrates how the persuasive power of facts can be perceived as dangerous and registered as "problematic." Clearly, the prospect of confronting one's own personal history in this case is an alarming experience. And, as always, the fear of the facts is stilled by a fascination with intellectual terms and abstractions aimed at concealing and masking the truth—the truth of facts that appear so threatening. Given that we do not deny it, and are prepared to face it, though, the truth of facts can help us to resolve our fears.

What is new is that the press's attempts to suppress the truth about childhood no longer go unchallenged. Here and there are enlightened witnesses who attempt to correct such destructive, anachronistic, but unfortunately, widespread opinions. In that sense, it would be wrong to claim that people who were once mistreated as children will have to remain in a state of ignorance their whole lives. There are now abundant examples of people who, on the contrary, with the help of an enlightened witness in childhood or later in life, have become conscious of the injustice done to them and, as a result, have acquired the capacity to empathize with others. To dismiss such people as "self-pitying" only says something about one's own early experiences—that no one took the suffering of children seriously and that the motto that governed the nursery read, "Pull yourself together." But when reviewers who grew up with this motto attempt to rule their little kingdoms by the same principle, thereby exposing their destructiveness, they will have to reckon with protests from those who are better informed.

One reader who, thanks to a helping witness, had been able to make her appalling, Prussian-style upbringing available to memory—an upbringing that didn't take place in the last century, but in the early fifties—sent me the following letter, which she had written to a leading weekly newspaper. It was a letter of outrage and justifiable anger. The newspaper answered it with silence. I would like to quote it here because it is representative of the views expressed to me by many people who wrote to me.

> *"What child wouldn't have cause to weep about its parents?" So wrote Nietzsche in* Thus Spake Zarathustra. *Recently, 60 percent of men, and 70 percent of women, questioned in a survey, admitted to having physically mistreated their children.*
>
> *The number of children subjected to sexual abuse—an estimated 300,000, though the figure is probably much higher—could also be found in the newspapers recently. Not in yours, however. In familiar, German-Prussian manner, you stuff its complaints back down the child's throat ("self-pitying" is the preferred phrase of arrogant, insensitive reviewers), and proceed to hit it across the head, noting on the way that Alice Miller has nothing to add to the "familiar knowledge" about child mistreatment. In your desolate, repressive intellectualism, you thereby turn yourself into an attorney for the greatest taboo on earth, an attorney for all masters of the art of denial, who euphemistically refer to the crimes committed against children as child abuse.*

From the letters I receive every day, I learn that the world has changed since I was a girl. Today, there are people prepared to counter mockery, lies, and ignorance, even in the public domain. Such letters also prove that it is no longer accurate to speak of the "German" manner. This now-united country also unites very different ways of being. The familiar, blind destroyers of life are still with us. But among them there are now informed witnesses, people who have done the necessary work on themselves and, for the first time in history, are doing everything they can to bring the whole truth about the mistreatment of children into the light of day.

PART TWO

Facts

6

Child Sacrifice as "Tradition"

STATISTICS SHOW THAT THERE ARE AT LEAST 74 million women alive today who had their clitorises removed before marriage.* What is involved here is an ancient custom, against which even African women are now protesting. Their protests, however, are usually met with outrage and threats—not only from men, but from other women, too. Why, one is tempted to ask, do women behave like this? Were they not themselves victims of this custom, based on the inhuman demand that women should not derive pleasure from the sexual act? Wouldn't African women wish to protect their daughters from this mutilation, from the brutal pain and the danger of infection, from which many women die? Obviously they would—were it not for the mechanisms enforcing the repression of anger, the mechanisms by which repressed anger is unconsciously projected onto the next generation.

The removal of a twelve-year-old girl's clitoris,

*Hanny Lightfoot-Klein, *Prisoners of Ritual* (Harrington Park Press, 1989), speaks about 100 million.

sometimes with, sometimes without anesthesia, is carried out by women who were once victims of the same procedure. Their consciousness, however, has not registered the realities of their situation. By repressing not only the pain but also their anger and desire for revenge, they have managed to banish consciousness, even idealizing the custom. Of course, they were unable to defend themselves as young girls and were forced to repress their feelings. Today, as a result of their repression, they can justify the procedure as harmless and necessary. They cannot recall their repressed anger and have never grieved about what happened to them. It was "a dictate of nature." Consequently, they inflict the same ordeal on their children without so much as wishing to acknowledge what they are doing to them.

One mother, charged with ruling on a case in which clitoridectomy had ended in her daughter's death, defended herself before a European court with the argument that without such an operation her daughter would never have been able to find a husband when she returned to her native land. The operation was, therefore, deemed as essential. Interviewed on television, the mother appeared to suspect no other possible motive for her behavior.

In the eyes of a European, that such a grave mutilation of young girls has been accepted for hundreds of years and continues to be practiced today appears as more or less incredible. Though Europeans have learned from an early age to give credence to nearly every other kind of lie, this is not one of them. They might well believe, for instance, that severity and discipline aimed at inducing a child's obedience results in the creation of a responsible and caring human being.

Impartial readers might nonetheless ask themselves: What in God's name can possibly be gained by shearing off the clitorises of millions of little girls?

Although it wouldn't lessen the hideousness of the custom, it would make more sense if it were the father who insisted on this female circumcision. Perhaps he once gratified his desire on the girl and wishes to deny the same favor to her future husband. Perhaps, by allowing his daughter to suffer, he is taking symbolic revenge on his mother. But what has God got to do with this custom? Why should God's will be advanced as a justification for settling such scores? Does God merely symbolize human interests? It is hard to find any other explanation. But why should God have such depraved motives for his commandments? And why, anyway, do human beings go on worshipping such horrific gods? To anyone who hasn't been circumcised—at least physically—the whole thing seems perfectly incomprehensible.

There are a number of reasons for such religiously sanctioned mistreatment of defenseless children; grown-up revenge for pain once suffered and subsequently repressed is not the only trigger. Unquestioning obedience to one's parents and the conviction passed on from them also allow such mutilation to go on flourishing as a tradition deemed worthy of preservation. Despite that, as reported in the magazine *Mothering* in 1987, there are, for instance, young Jewish people in the United States who, though religious themselves, reject circumcision as a matter of principle because they have come to see its horrendousness.

In *Banished Knowledge* I cited in detail the naturalist Desmond Morris. He has proved that none of the so-called scientific arguments for circumcision holds water. This has been substantiated by research in England and America. On the contrary, circumcision is a fashion, a fashion that plays on the ignorance and gullibility of the public, and from which doctors earn handsome dividends. Now that insurance companies have stopped paying for it, however, this fashion is rapidly losing its appeal. Even talk of its medical necessity has visibly dried up.

The temptation to ward off the comprehensible, but deadly desire for revenge—a desire previously repressed—for the brutalization suffered in one's own childhood is so powerful that it is immune to moral injunction. The situation is abetted by religion, which is instrumental in sanctioning this kind of human sacrifice and even blessing it. Only by becoming conscious of this justifiable rage and the desire for revenge can new crimes be prevented and the vicious circle of ignorance broken. As soon as a circumcised woman is capable of facing the shockingly sad fact that she was used by her parents as a sacrificial lamb in a pointless religious ritual, she will no longer wish to inflict the same on her daughter. She will know whose name is on that anger and not require an innocent child to atone for the crimes once committed against her by others. Even if the appalling custom of clitoridectomy does not occur in our culture, countless other people have had to undergo an equivalent amputation—that of their sensory and emotional world, hideously mutilated by mistreatment and cruel child rearing.

The thousands years' old tradition of child abuse and child murder will not be stopped overnight. The word "tradition" has a pleasant ring to it. This year, in neutral Switzerland—a country that has never waged a war of aggression and whose army exists for purely defensive purposes—a referendum was held, in harmony with the general mood of disarmament in Europe, on the question of whether the army should be completely disbanded. Interviewed on the street, an old man insisted that the army should at all costs be maintained—for the sake of "tradition." He could have said: "Who knows whether our neighbors might one day think differently than they do today? We can't be dependent on the political vagaries of the more powerful countries around us. Our independence is too vital to take any risks." He didn't say that, however. He simply said: one should maintain such a costly army out of tradition. And the person who posed the question evidently found nothing remarkable in this view.

Many people have similar views about the disciplining of children. Beating children and inflicting ritual horrors on them is, they say, a question of tradition. It was also "tradition" in China for girls to have their feet mutilated and bandaged. And because it has been "tradition" to kill people, we have been waging war for thousands of years. Today, we are at a turning point in our history. We can no longer continue to accept tradition for tradition's sake. We can no longer go on playing the same old war games without eventually becoming conscious of the dimensions of the destruction involved. We must realize that child murder was also part of our "traditions" and that our blindness in respect of this tradition is itself a consequence of this practice. We have no other choice but to become fully conscious of the darker aspects of our own cultural heritage. Only then will we cease to pass them blindly on to future generations.

7

The Monstrous Consequences of Denial

ADOLF HITLER'S PATH TO GENOCIDE*

> *"What luck for those in power that people don't think."*
>
> —JOACHIM FEST, *Hitler*, 1973

CAN ONE, IN TODAY'S GERMANY, STILL DISPUTE the fact that there would never have been a Hitler, or Hitler supporters, if there had been no child abuse, if children had not been brought up, with the help of violence, to blindly obey? And that millions would not have been murdered? Probably every thinking person in postwar Germany has, at one time or another, posed the question: How could a human being have conceived and built a gigantic killing machine—and found millions of helpers to set it in motion?

The monster Adolf Hitler, murderer of millions, master of destruction and organized insanity, was not in

*Parts of this section were published in a special issue of the magazine *Der Spiegel*.

fact born a monster. Neither was he sent by the devil, as most people think. He did not fall from the sky to bring "order" to Germany, build its autobahns, and lead it out of economic depression, as some people still believe today. He was not born with "destructive drives," because there are no such things; our biological purpose is to maintain life, not destroy it. A person is never born destructive and we are *by nature* neither good nor bad. How we deploy our abilities depends on our character. This is formed in the course of our lives and determined by our individual experiences, above all those in childhood and youth, and the decisions we make as adults.

Hitler, like every other child, was born innocent. Like many other children at that time, he was destructively raised by his parents. Later, he would become a monster. He was a survivor of that engine of destruction known in turn-of-the-century Germany as child rearing. It was what I call the hidden concentration camp of childhood, the one that may never be brought to light.

How this insidious horror could turn into the manifest horror of Hitler's Third Reich I have described in detail in my book *For Your Own Good* and in my subsequent books *Banished Knowledge* and *The Untouched Key*. There, too, can be found a complete presentation of the evidence for everything that I will here only outline.

Every abused child must totally repress the mistreatment, confusion, and neglect it suffered. If it were not to do so, it would die. The child's organism could not withstand the dimensions of this pain. Only in adulthood do other ways of handling our feelings become available to us. If we do not make use of these opportunities, then what was once the life-saving function of repression can turn into a dangerous, destructive, and self-destructive power. The careers of such tyrants as Hitler or Stalin show how previously suppressed revenge fantasies can lead to destructive actions of near-indescribable proportions. We do not encounter this phenomenon in the animal kingdom because no young animal will ever be trained by its parents to such a complete denial of its nature in order to make of it a "good" animal. Only human beings behave so destructively. Descriptions of the childhoods of Nazi criminals, and of Vietnam volunteers, the Green Berets, show that mindless programming to destructiveness always begins with a brutal upbringing aimed at enforcing unthinking obedience and total contempt for the child.

The Auschwitz commandant Rudolf Höss has, for instance, tellingly characterized his childhood—albeit without perceiving in it the roots of his inhumanity (see R. Höss, *Der Kommandant von Auschwitz*, Munich, 1963):

> *Above all, I was constantly reminded that I was to comply with, and follow, the wishes or commands of parents, teachers, priests, etc., indeed all grown-ups including the servants, and that I was to allow nothing to distract me from that duty. Whatever they said, went. These fundamental values of my upbringing became part of my flesh and blood.*

To suppress the feelings, perceptions, and impulses of a child is to commit psychic murder. The experiences Höss went through in his youth gave him a thorough grounding in the grammar of death. He simply had to wait thirty years, whereupon Hitler's regime presented him with the opportunity to practice the skills he had learned.

Thousands of his contemporaries functioned in just the same way. Instead of exposing and condemning the criminal behavior of their parents, they uniformly praised and defended it. Had a consciousness of the absurdity and dangerousness of brutal child rearing already existed, monsters like Höss could never have been possible. The susceptibility to blind obedience and *the demand for a man like Hitler simply would not have existed in Germany*.

The young people who demonstrated in Central and Eastern Europe against the lies of their governments and for more freedom had certainly grown up to something other than obedience and hypocrisy. The change in their upbringing was proved by the fact that they were capable of standing up for their rights without damaging their cause by blind, uncontrolled destructiveness, as had been the case with the terrorists in the sixties. The upbringing of those terrorists was steeped in cruel educational theories. To achieve their supposedly humanitarian ends, they, like their parents before them, chose brutal violence as their means. The young people demonstrating in 1989 were capable of exposing the emptiness, terror, mendacity, and destructiveness of Stalinism—all the things with which their parents and grandparents came to terms—because as children they were allowed more freedom than the older generation. To be conscious of unfreedom one must have a concept of what freedom and respect for life are.

A person who has never experienced this as a child, who has only known and been exposed to extreme violence, brutality, and hypocrisy, without ever having come across a single helping witness, does not demonstrate for freedom. Such a person demands order and uses violence to achieve it, just as he or she learned as a child: order and cleanliness at any price is the motto, even if it is at the price of life. The victims of such an upbringing ache to do to others what was once done to them. If they don't have children, or their children refuse to make themselves available for their revenge, they line up to support new forms of fascism. Ultimately, fascism always has the same goal: the annihilation of truth and freedom. People who have been mistreated as children, but totally deny their suffering, use the mottoes and labels of the day. They thereby meet the approval of others like them because they are also helping to conceal their truth. They are consumed by the perverse pleasure in the destruction of life that they observed in their parents when young. They long to at last be on the other side of the fence, to hold power themselves, passing it off, as Stalin, Hitler, or Ceausescu have done, as "redemption" for others. This old childhood longing determines their political "opinions" and speeches, which are therefore impervious to counter-arguments. As long as they continue to ignore or distort the roots of the problem, which lie in the very real threats experienced in their childhood, reason must remain impotent against this kind of persecution complex. *The unconscious compulsion to revenge repressed injuries is more powerful than all reason.* That is the lesson that all tyrants teach us. One should not expect judiciousness from a mad person motivated by compulsive panic. One should, however, protect oneself from such a person.

It is our access to the truth that can enable us to prevent such people, who yearn for the "order" spawned by violence, from realizing their destructive plans. Fascism will have had its day once society ceases to deny the knowledge we already possess about the production of brutality, violence, and dehumanization in childhood and minimize its dangers. Once this has happened, it won't have a chance in this society. It is not enough to unmask Stalinism and Nazism as mere lies. As long as we do not recognize the circumstances to which they owe their success, these and similar lies can continue to exist, dressed up in forms in keeping with the "Zeitgeist." Fascism is a psychic attitude that floats the latent history of destruction to the surface.

The nature of fascism is not determined by political

or economic circumstances. For a long time, people sought to "explain" Hitler's success by pointing to the catastrophic economic situation of the Weimar Republic, and in doing so they sought to collectively deny the origins of Hitler's urge toward revenge, destruction, and power. But we eventually desperately need the truth.

It is not enough to see the surface and describe that. We have to recognize, and defuse, the *production* of paranoid confusion, which takes place in childhood. Clear, firm legislation, which would unequivocally condemn the mistreatment of children as a crime, would be a first, decisive step in the right direction (see chapter 9).

Access to the truth of our own history would enable us to clearly see that what a few destructive and confused people wish to realize—however attractive and reasonable it might sound to all those who have shared the same fate—is nothing less than hell, the hell that they themselves escaped, a hell of cynicism, arrogance, brutality, destructive rage, and stupidity. Denial is the ladder out of this hell, enabling them to emerge with the burning desire to finally revenge themselves for it.

Can one have a dialogue with such people? I believe we must keep trying because this may, indeed it very likely will, be their first opportunity of encountering an enlightened witness. How they make use of this encounter is something over which we have no influence. But we should at least make use of the occasion. Life failed them—something that is, I suspect, true of all prison inmates. One should try to show them that they had the right to respect, love, and encouragement in their childhood and that this right was denied them, but that this does not give them the right to destroy the lives of others. We must also show them that destruction is a dead end. Even millions of corpses could not sate Hitler's hunger for revenge or dispel his hatred. We have to show them that what was passed off on them in childhood as "a good upbringing" was a base, mendacious, and idiotic ideology in which they had to believe in order to survive, and that they now wish to recirculate at the political level. And we have to show them that the people who cheated them, who engendered their misery, their hunger for power and destruction, were not Jews or Turks or Arabs or Gypsies, but their very own parents—clean, orderly citizens, God-fearing, respectable churchgoers.

We cannot know how many of these sons and daughters, how many young neo-fascists or violent criminals are open to dialogue. But if we bear in mind that in our society they hardly ever come across someone who enlightens them about this horrendous truth, then it is conceivable that one or the other of them might pause to listen. It may be that the evidence of facts that they know from their own childhood, but were never allowed to see in context, will immediately become clear to them, especially if they have not spent years at a university learning how to deny and disguise such facts.

The danger does not lie with individuals, however criminal they may be. Far more, it lies in the ignorance of our entire society, which *confirms these people in the lies that they were obliged to believe in their childhood.* Teachers, attorneys, doctors, social workers, priests, and other respected representatives of society protect parents from the mistreated child's every accusation and see to it that the truth about child abuse remains concealed. Even the child protection agencies insist that this crime, and this crime alone, should go unpunished (see *Banished Knowledge*, p. 127).

But it is precisely the correct information about the mistreatment of children, which brings in its wake further abuse, that could help us to avert the dangers that threaten us. Among other things, we could ensure that children who have been seriously mistreated and have, as a result, turned into paranoid criminals, never become leaders of entire nations or gain the power to control and destroy millions of people. In Nero's time, it was a person's inevitable fate to live under the tyranny of one individual, but in the age of democracy, however imperfect it may be, it is in the hands of the voter to abrogate such a fate. We can choose blindness or the truth of facts. Whoever opts for the truth will not deliver himself to people who promise redemption by the destruction of others. He or she will know that this hunger for destruction is not an inherent, primal need that can at some point be stilled. Rather, it is a permanent, perverted search for revenge, which would ultimately affect those who voted for such tyrants, should they not find the necessary courage to reinstate the truth.

I know of no example that is so well documented and so clearly illustrates the consequences of child murder—one of them being the resultant collective blindness—than the calamitous success of Adolf Hitler.

On one occasion Hitler related to his secretary how, during one of the routine beatings that his father gave him, he had managed to stop himself from crying, to feel nothing and even count the thirty-two strokes received (see John Toland, *Adolf Hitler*, Lübbe, 1977). It was in this way—through the total denial of his pain, his feelings of powerlessness and desperation; that is, through the denial of the truth—that Hitler fashioned himself into the master of violence and inhuman cynicism that he became. The result was a primitive human being, incapable of empathy for other human beings. He was without mercy. The feelings of hate and revenge latent in him constantly drove him to new acts of destruction. Then, when millions of people had been condemned to death through these actions caused by his feelings, the feelings he had repressed and denied returned to persecute him in his sleep. Hermann Rauschning has described the Führer's nocturnal screaming attacks that were invariably accompanied by "indecipherable counting." The origins of these habits, I believe, lie in the punitive rituals of his childhood (see *For Your Own Good*, p. 173).

Hitler did not invent fascism. Like so many of his contemporaries, he found it ready-made in the totalitarian regime of his home. The Nazi formulation of fascism bears unmistakable traces of Hitler's childhood. But the underlying principles of his upbringing were in no way exceptional. Consequently, neither Gerhard Hauptmann, Martin Heidegger, nor numerous other brilliant intellectuals, raised according to the same principles, were able to see through Hitler's madness. To be able to do so they would have had to be able to see through the madness of their own childhoods.

Adolf Hitler was given the opportunity to turn Europe and the rest of the world into the battlefield of his childhood because there were so many millions of people in Germany at that time who had experienced similar things in their first year of life. The following principles were for them, though not necessarily at the conscious level, self-evident:

1. Obedience and order, not life, are the highest values.
2. Only by recourse to violence can order be established and maintained.
3. Creativity, as embodied in children, is a danger to adults and must be destroyed.
4. Absolute obedience to the father is the ultimate arbiter.
5. Disobedience and criticism are unthinkable, because they will be punished with corporal punishment and death threats.

6. The lively, vital child should be turned, as early as possible, into an obedient robot and slave.
7. Unwelcome feelings and real needs must, consequently, be suppressed to the maximum.
8. A mother is never to take the side of her child against the father's disciplinary measures. On the contrary, after the particular torture has been carried out, she should preach deference and love of its parents to the child.

Fortunately, there were people here and there with whom the child could find refuge from this totalitarian regime, and even experience love, respect, and protection. Thanks to these positive experiences—if nothing else, they provided contrast—the child could at least internally condemn the horrors it went through and not begin to develop the wish to later become the tormentor of others. But in the absence of any such redeeming witnesses, the child had, in this bizarre scenario, no other choice but to suppress every kind of natural reflex, such as anger or even laughter. It also had to practice constant obedience. Only thus could it hope to keep the threat posed by its father within bearable limits. This early character drilling was later exploited by Hitler. In almost exact imitation of the pedagogic system that he had come to know firsthand as a child, he proceeded to fashion the ideology of Nazism. What that looked like in practice was:

1. The will of the Führer is the ultimate law.
2. The Führer will create order by force, turning Germany into a paradise for Aryans—that is, the master race.
3. Whoever submits to his orders like a robot will be rewarded.

4. Whoever dares to criticize the system has to go to a concentration camp.
5. Jews, Gypsies, homosexuals, and followers of religious sects are to be destroyed—men, women, and children included.
6. Poles and Russians are to become useable slaves.
7. The handicapped and mentally ill are also to be killed.
8. Artistic freedom is dangerous. "Decadent" art, as every other kind of creativity, should be hunted down.

If it weren't for the numerous documentary films that bear witness to the jubilation of the masses, nobody would today believe that a madman with such an antihuman ideology could call forth such enthusiasm. How was it actually possible that Hitler could find such an enormous following? Was it that he promised the people a solution to all their problems and offered them a convenient scapegoat? This was certainly so. But that would not have been sufficient to make countless people allow themselves to be used as puppets. This promise had to be given in the style of the power-hungry, violent father that most of them knew, feared, and admired.

The history of human sacrifice and cannibalism, as far back as the Aztecs, shows us how different religions have sanctified human sacrifice in order to gloss over the crimes of parents against their children. Anyone who reads this history with open eyes again and again encounters the same pattern: "If I inflict on others what was once inflicted on me, I don't have to feel the pain that memory would bring. If I skillfully dress everything up with ideology or religion and keep telling the lies which those around me have learned to believe in, then many people will follow me. If I can also—like Hitler—employ the talents of an actor and take on the allure of the threatening father, the father that nearly everyone totally believed and feared in childhood, then I can find countless helpers for every possible kind of crime, the more absurd, the easier." This has been amply proved by the Milgram test.* Many grown-ups, yesterday's obedient children, are only waiting for a legalized outlet for the rage suppressed in them for decades. In the maltreatment of their own children, commonly known as "child rearing," in wars or acts of genocide, society offers them this outlet and the appropriate justification specific to their own culture.

Not least in our recent history have been the lessons of *the dangers of our traditional moral values*. We are urged to honor our parents and never question them, whatever they have done. But when I realize that millions of people had to die so that Adolf Hitler could keep his repression intact, that millions were humiliated in camps, so that he should never feel how he was once humiliated, then I have to say: we cannot point out these connections often enough or clearly enough so that the mindless production of evil can be made transparent. How are young people supposed to be able to recognize and condemn inhumanity and crimes if such things as medical experiments on humans go on being concealed instead of revealed in the greatest possible clarity?

Had the deeds of the big, and the little, Mengeles not remained hidden behind a solid wall of silence for the last forty years, similar phenomena could be recognized far quicker than they are today. Unfortunately, only very few people benefit from present discoveries. As

*The Milgram test demonstrated the correlation between violence and blind obedience to authority. The persons tested were asked to punish pupils for a mistake they had made by administering what the testers described as (but were not in fact) electric shocks of growing intensity. Regardless of the screams of the "victims," 62 percent of the people tested continued the punishment, administering shocks up to a voltage of 450. They did not dare to protest against this cruel order.

a result, it is still possible to justify hideous experiments on defenseless people in the name of scientific freedom and their "benefit to mankind" without arousing the slightest public outrage.

Only if young people are allowed to know exactly what happened and why, if they no longer allow themselves to be deflected in their curiosity and do not fear the truth, can they free themselves from the burden of their forefathers' blindness. Such young people will certainly not condone the production of poisoned gas.

Hitler's story warns us against blindness and exhorts us, at last, to give it up and struggle against collective repression. I strive to do this in all my books, in order to bring home the psychodynamics of child abuse and its immeasurable consequences for our society, as revealed by Hitler's life. I am convinced that once the name Hitler is no longer surrounded by taboo, the story of his childhood and life will contribute a great deal to our understanding and prevention of similar catastrophes, now and in the future. It goes without saying that this attempt to understand someone like Hitler in no way means pitying someone as pitiless as he.

The greatest obstacle on this long journey is the denial of our own childhood mistreatment and our defense against it at the expense of our children, subordinates, partners, or voters. In 1987 more than half of all parents in West Germany still registered their approval of beatings as an appropriate pedagogic means. And this, despite the many years of educative work carried out by child protection agencies. Where does this stubborn mindlessness come from? Why don't these parents know that physical violence and also psychic "beatings" mean mistreatment and humiliation of a child, which will sooner or later break through in open or concealed form? Why don't they know that with their demonstrably false assertion that beating a child is both absolutely necessary and perfectly harmless, they are condoning, maintaining, and continuing a destructive tradition? They didn't know it, of course, because they are really familiar with this kind of child rearing from their own experience. Early on they were taught to regard it as normal and harmless. Violence is, in the eyes of such parents, the only effective means of correcting a child's behavior. For that reason this generation of parents constructs elaborate theories to explain away the mass murder of the Third Reich and their parents' own passive complicity. That seems to them easier than allowing themselves to experience the pain of their own early humiliations as abused children. But they ignore the price they and their children have to pay for this avoidance. Were they to feel that truth, they could gain access to the key to understanding, the understanding that would protect their children from abuse and protect them from their own blindness as parents and voters. If they were politicians, this realization might protect whole nations, and their victims, from senseless wars.

Conventional wars have claimed the lives of countless people. National leaders intent on war do not want to believe that the destructive forces from which they constantly attempt to free themselves at other people's expense are in themselves revenge feelings for old, very personal wounds. In the face of even the possibility of nuclear war, we simply cannot afford to go on ignoring this fact. But that is exactly what we do: numerous civil servants and government specialists deal with the results of child abuse, without being able to see and know its origins.

But even the most desolate of childhoods does not justify the criminals' destruction of human life. As adults, they have the chance of facing their past. They can stop denying the horrendousness of that time, experience their formerly repressed hatred, and seek to understand its causes. Hatred experienced consciously is only a feeling, after all, and feelings can't kill. Blind, destructive actions carried out against substitute victims can, by contrast, cost human life. There is no excuse for such actions. But who knows? Perhaps our grandchildren will be able to say of their lives: "How lucky we are that we weren't beaten like our grandparents and can therefore see things more clearly than they could. If hitting a child were really as harmless as they say, then people would not have been blind to Hitler's crimes against humanity. They would have seen through them immediately and rejected them, as our children do today when faced with monstrousness."

Children who are allowed to defend themselves will not be destructive. Destructiveness—the phenomenon that governs our world—is not our ineluctable fate. If we love and care for our children, it can be banished from the face of the earth. The "urge to destruction" slumbers only in the victims of childhood mistreatment, who as adults do not want to know what happened in their early life. Adults not mistreated in childhood do not feel the need to mistreat their defenseless children. They can't even imagine it, even when they are nervous and stressed and therefore respond to challenging queries with impatience. There are so many other ways to relate to children—productive, respectful, and creative ways. Even less imaginable than the need for revenge against their children is the idea that they might have become fascinated by a monster like Hitler. People who have been respected in childhood, who have not been drilled by abuse and mistreatment into robots, will never be prepared to die out of "obedience to the Führer"; nor will they, against all reason, dispatch thousands to their deaths in Stalingrad, simply because some lunatic has come up with the idea.

Hitler's generals, by contrast, stood at attention when he entered his headquarters. All objections that could have been raised were consumed by fear and mental paralysis, enthusiasm even, when they heard HIM (their fathers) speak. This political blindness, which cost the lives of millions of people, proves precisely what our grandparents so energetically contested: that in every case, physical as well as psychic abuse of a child not only causes damage, but also places the child in the greatest danger in later life: that is, it makes the child susceptible to destructiveness. And that applies not only to individuals. Under certain circumstances, it can be true of entire nations. Rumania's recent history provides new and tragic proof of this fact.

NICOLAE CEAUSESCU'S VISION OF REDEMPTION

Disguising and transforming his own identity was one of the driving forces of his life. Hardly any other historical figure has stylized himself with such violence and pedantic determination or made the real nature of his person so invisible. The conception he had of himself resembles a monument far more than it resembles a person, a monument behind which he spent his whole life trying to conceal himself.

—JOACHIM FEST, *Hitler*, 1973

I cited this passage from Joachim Fest's book about Hitler ten years ago in my book *For Your Own Good*, noting: "Someone who has experienced his mother's love will never need to disguise himself in this way." At the end of 1989 we once again found ourselves confronted by a very similar phenomenon. In view of Nicolae Ceausescu's character we can no longer claim "that hardly any other historical figure has stylized himself . . . or made the real nature of his person so invisible" as Hitler. How many more victims will be necessary until we have got it into our heads what these "stylized monuments" produce?

In 1973, at the death of Ceausescu's father at the age of eighty, the Communist dictator summoned a bishop and twelve other members of the clergy to the consecration out of respect for his parents' religiosity. Ceausescu's contemporaries bear witness to his deep respect and fidelity to his parents. Which is not to say that his parents in any way treated him with love and respect. But children who have been mistreated stand out by virtue of their pronounced dependency, thralldom, and absence of criticism. In Ceausescu's case what it meant was that the dictator had totally repressed the mistreatment he had suffered in childhood—at the expense of the entire Rumanian people.

He let men, women, and children freeze and starve not simply because he himself once suffered terrible poverty, but because he was raised with hypocrisy and mistreatments—and totally denied his past. Numerous people have grown up in poverty. Nonetheless, they do not all feel the need to make others suffer—especially if they came into contact with loving and honest human beings when they were children. For instance, actor Charlie Chaplin's mother, herself a single parent, was also poor; and Chaplin himself spent some of his childhood in an almshouse in which hideous practices were the rule. But he had a mother who loved him and who did not abandon him even when he was in the institution. This early experience of love, coupled with sadness and wistfulness, can be felt in most of his films.

Ceausescu's father, on the other hand, was not only poor and the father of ten children, one of whom died young. He spent what little money he had on drinking bouts instead of feeding his children; he also beat them daily "for their own good." So did the fathers of Hitler and Stalin, both of whom, though to differing degrees, were frequently drunk—Stalin's was a chronic alcoholic; Hitler's, a serious drinker. Ceausescu's mother, although illiterate, was ambitious and closely monitored her children's school grades. She, too, beat them continually. As the parents, above all the mother, were both very religious, they always had a fine "moral" justification for their behavior at the ready. Ceausescu, consequently, never questioned the rightness of this physical abuse. From the beginning, hypocrisy hung heavy in the air he breathed. Thus he regarded it as quite normal.

The repressed rage that he carried within him—and which he himself did not comprehend—could at first only find an outlet in the killing of young animals. He was known for such behavior both as a child in the village and, later, as a teenager, in prison. His cellmates, who were considerably older than he, reported how on one occasion he strangled the newborn kittens of a stray cat.

But such small acts of revenge were not enough to work off the hypocrisy and cruelty stored in him. In puberty, he finally found in the Communist Party the appropriate ideology. Later it would allow him to enact on the political stage what he had learned in childhood. Just as his parents had once pretended to beat him for his own good, so he would now claim to "redeem" the Rumanian nation with the help of imprisonment, brainwashing, humiliation, and the suppression of the truth.

In a biography of the dictator (see Heinz Siegert, *Ceausescu*, Munich, 1973, p. 78ff), the following is reported:

> *Nicolae Ceausescu was born on January 26, 1918. Little authentic evidence is available about his childhood. The chairman of the local town council will not*

speak about it. Family members are similarly reticent. People don't wish to make a to-do about this period of his life.

When Nicolae Ceausescu was a child, only one room could be heated in the family house and the whole family had to crowd into it. There were no beds and no furniture, as there wouldn't have been any room for them. Ranged along the walls were plank beds covered with rush mattresses on which the whole family slept together. . . . In Ceausescu's family there were two children with the same name: one is the Nicolae who is today the President of Rumania; the other Nicolae was the youngest of the ten children, for whom the parents couldn't even be bothered to find a different name. . . .

The world into which Nicolae Ceausescu was born as the third child of Rumanian peasants was a grim one. The farming country, as it existed in Rumania until after the Second World War, was unlike any other European country. At best, the poverty of Rumania's rural population could be compared with that of South American states. For the landless or the small subsistence farmers, bread was only available once a week. For millions of people, mamaliga, a porridge made of maize, was the staple food. That was also true of the family of Andruza Ceausescu in the little Oltonian village of Scornicesti. In drought years, which came with crippling regularity, supplies were not even sufficient for this meagre meal. . . .

Infant mortality was high. Even as late as 1930 nearly a fifth of all new-born babies died in infancy.

I asked Ceausescu's biographer how the dictator, who struck me, in his appearance on television, as unfeeling and masklike, had seemed to him twenty years before. The author, who had interviewed him at that time as well as visiting his birthplace, told me that absolutely nothing factual was known about him. The moment the interviewer asked for facts—about Ceausescu's childhood, for instance—and wouldn't permit himself to be fobbed off with ideological platitudes about "blossoming Rumania," he felt an indomitable wall go up between him and the dictator. In conversation, Ceausescu was stiff and distrustful. He never laughed. Only when photographers were around did he put on his artificial smile.

The deeper Ceausescu repressed the memory of his father's violent recklessness, the more visibly his own son Niku's alcohol addiction raged. One of the young man's party tricks was to throw unopened bottles of whiskey within millimeters of people's heads and watch them shatter against the wall (see Ion Pacepa, *Horizons Rouges*, Paris, 1987).

Anyone who has followed the news about Rumania on television in recent years recalls the dictator's characteristic hand gesture, reminiscent of the motions of a windshield wiper. Watching this gesture I sometimes had the impression of a person trying to wipe out memories—to erase facts, so as to be able to carry on down the road, even as more and more fears settle on his field of vision like troublesome insects. The raised hand with which Ceausescu continually saluted the masses reminded me of the hand of an adult raised at the moment before he lands a blow on his child (his loyal people!). The raised arm of the "Heil Hitler" salute doubtless has the same origins. The repressed fear of all dictators talks through their body language.

Unfortunately, the tyrant's gestures were not the only place that the repressed misery of Ceausescu's childhood found expression. His leadership brought to light everything that the nine surviving Ceausescu children had banished to the twilight of forgetfulness and on no account wished to know—such as, for instance, the total control that, packed like sardines into a single, tiny room, they could never escape; or the hypocrisy of their religious upbringing and the idiocy of their parents having children they could not cope with and to whom they only had impatience, misery, and lovelessness to offer.

A free child might have asked: Why do our parents go on having children, when they can't even feed them, keep them warm or pay them any attention, when they can't even remember their names? But a mistreated child cannot ask such questions. It believes what it has been taught to believe: that God wanted these children. Is God, then, responsible for all the unwanted, mistreated, and neglected children in the world? Does he enjoy watching millions of children starve or freeze to death? As we all know, God's wishes are not open to query. One simply has to obey them, however absurd they may seem. Many devout believers assume that behind such wishes, there must be some hidden meaning to which we have no access (see chapter 8). Ceausescu never really questioned his childhood, his parents, or what that "God" meant to him. Very likely he saw in himself a messenger of God's will. Otherwise, the "Carpathian genius" would not have forced his people to go on bearing children who would end up living in misery.

As Ceausescu, aided by Communist ideology, came to power, he presented himself as "a God with inordinate wishes." He brought down on the entire Rumanian people the fate that had once been his own: a superfluity of children, enforced by the insane whim of a godlike dictator, children one could neither feed nor keep warm.

As priests and the confession box had seen to the upholding of God's dictates in Scornicesti, so the "Securitate," Ceausescu's secret police, were enjoined to watch over and check the wombs of Rumanian women. They were to see to it that the dictator's godlike "wish for a nation of families teeming with children"—children who would then freeze to death—was fulfilled. Nor were women, on any account, to have time to devote themselves to their children. Enforced births would see to that. They were to have it no different than Ceausescu's own mother, who, compelled by an alcoholic to conception after conception, had no choice but to let her children grow up in misery and want. By proxy, the tyrant revenged himself for his personal fate on thousands of mothers, fathers, and children. Because he refused to face his destiny, keeping his story and feelings from that time completely repressed, he drove an entire people to the brink of destruction.

Ceausescu not only drove Rumanian children into the same misery as was once his own: lovelessness, hunger, cold, total control, and all-pervasive hypocrisy. With the help of the women of Rumania he also sought to take unconscious revenge on his mother. *Consciously* he never ceased to glorify her, but by forcing millions of Rumanian women to become mothers, he could reinforce his repression. He would never have to feel what he had repressed as a child: that he was nothing but a burden to his mother and that she literally forgot—and this can be verified—that he even existed.

Today, we know what remained hidden for so long: that the campaign to increase the birth rate, orchestrated by the secret police in the early 1970s, cost the lives of thousands and thousands of mothers and children. The most common cause of death for the mothers was infection. Doctors who undertook abortions risked their names being stricken from the register of practicing physicians and a seven-year jail sentence. In many cases, they were only allowed to attend to women brought into hospital with often fatal injuries—the result of illegal, "back-street" abortions—if they cooperated with the police by naming names. Refusal to do so would cost them their lives. Such facts make it clear that the dictator specialized in having the entire country spied on and persecuted. For Ceausescu, such total control was all part of a day's work.

In the middle of January 1990, a German television network reported for the first time of a children's ward in a hospital in Temesvar, referred to by the staff as "the Auschwitz ward." People in the region would only refer to the ward in whispers. In this clinic, sick or undernourished babies were left to vegetate—and this at the personal command of Ceausescu himself. The children's conditions were reminiscent of those of babies from the worst starvation zones of the Third World. They were intentionally neglected and mostly lay two to an incubator. The incubator itself was only heated if the power supply had not been cut—otherwise the children had to lie virtually unprotected at external temperatures of as little as 25° below zero, consigned to death under the watchful eye of doctors and nurses. Condemning doctors and nurses to become the passive witnesses of dying children is part of the scenario of repressed history. Were Ceausescu's parents not also witness to the pain and misery of their children, while denying their responsibility for it?

In *For Your Own Good*, I was able to show in detail what kind of "logic" stood behind the inhuman laws of the Third Reich. I was able to show that the presence of a schizophrenic aunt who lived under the same roof throughout Hitler's childhood had a considerable influence on the framing of his gruesome "euthanasia" legislation. To me, it is also revealing that suspicion of his illegitimate father's Jewish ancestry inflamed Hitler's obsessive hatred of the Jews. At the conscious level, of course, he expressed hatred of neither father nor aunt.

There are still some admirers of Hitler alive today. Many still refuse to accept such realizations and learn from history. They refuse to face reality and wish to cling to "rational" explanations of Hitler's so-called politics. In Ceausescu's case it might be somewhat different. He had neither supporters nor admirers. He was an absurd, self-elected god. The "Securitate" was his priesthood. His fall from power led to the dissolution of this "church." What remains are the sufferings of a people who had been terrorized for decades; one can only hope that these sufferings will be confronted and not repressed. Also remaining is a long shiver of fear.

But we won't be able to avoid similar catastrophes in the future if we merely rest in fear. Our understanding of how such a thing could happen—because given similar circumstances, it could indeed happen again—is crucial if we are not to simply go on as before.

Ceausescu's deeds show, just as do the deeds of Hitler, Stalin, and other tyrants, that from the beginning, his political career was governed by the idea of *redemption through destruction*. No one who has not been tortured and betrayed in childhood will turn into a dictator. Ceausescu must have constantly had it drummed into him as a child that he was beaten, tortured, and spied on, that his soul was plundered, for his own good, without ever being able to see through the lie. These unexposed lies later become the fundamental principles of the tyrant.

Without a helping witness a mistreated child does not regard the damage done to its integrity as psychic mutilation. It believes that its father truly wanted something positive as he beat it. The leader of the Front National in France, for instance, speaking on television, declared his support of corporal punishment for children and went on to say how much he owed the beatings his father and grandfather had given him as a child. Such opinions are, in fact, not surprising. They follow a logic of their own. A mistreated child *must* repress all doubt to survive. If it were to doubt the benevolent purpose of what it suffered, it would place itself in mortal danger.

But where does such repression lead an adult who refuses to give it up? As we can learn by the example of all dictators, the belief forms and takes hold that if they do to the people what their parents once did to them—that is, humiliate and dominate, enslave, exploit, mock, and silence them—they will be redeeming them. Then it is a question of how alert that people is: whether it behaves with the naïveté of the seven billy goats in the Grimm brothers' fairy tale, who fall for the wolf's white paws and confuse it with their mother, or whether they have learned enough from the history of other peoples to know that *the planned destruction of life, of freedom, truth and people themselves has never led to salvation*.

Because of a long tradition, which makes it seem almost self-evident, this absurd coupling of redemption and destruction goes unnoticed by the majority of people. Even in the Song of Solomon we can read, "he who spares the rod, spoils the boy." Thus, the connection between supposed love and "redemption" through destruction and cruelty is already established in the Old Testament as god-given. At his trial, the peasant's son, Ceausescu, said that he had destroyed eight thousand beautiful, ancient villages only to build hospitals and schools for the people. Actually, the same people had to freeze and starve so that the "great, good-natured father" could build palaces for himself. In a similar way, little Nicolae and his brothers and sisters had had to endure cold and starvation so that their irresponsible father could pay for his schnapps in the local bar.

Although I could vividly imagine the origins of the dictator's evident mendacity, I wished to give facts in this book that would illustrate these origins. I therefore searched for further information about the childhood of the person who had proved his barely credible mania for destruction right before our eyes. Most of the journalists, historians, and political scientists to whom I spoke understandably knew nothing about Ceausescu's childhood. They weren't interested in the subject. A few journalists, who had lived for a number of years in Bucharest, passed on to me various rumors without being able to verify them independently. One rumor held, for instance, that the fifteen-year-old apprentice shoemaker roamed around the main railway station, stealing. On one occasion, it seems, he stole a suitcase full of Marxist literature. This, I was told, was his first contact with the Communist Party. Whether the ensuing prison sentence is to be ascribed to the theft or his membership in the Communist Party, as the official biographies claim, is a moot point. What is certain is that he was imprisoned for many years and that he accepted those harsh prison years, including frequent torture and denial of food, without the slightest emotional protest.

Even if this is the dictator's own version of his story, it nonetheless reflects the pride of the once-abused child in its capacity to repress and deny feelings—a pride that we are already familiar with from

Adolf Hitler. In both cases, it led to the blocking and destruction of every kind of empathy with others. Ceausescu's "equanimity" in prison, which has been confirmed by other prison inmates, was itself the result of earlier, repressed mistreatment in childhood.

To my question as to how a brother could also be christened Nicolae, I repeatedly received the reply that the father was drunk "as usual" at the time the child was named. By all accounts, he had simply forgotten that he already had a son named Nicolae—though no one could explain to me how Ceausescu's mother could also forget that fact. This information seemed to arouse little surprise in Bucharest. But without a doubt it throws light on the dictator's obsessive desire for revenge. This was none other than the absurd and insatiable determination to gain at last the recognition completely denied him as a child. Had it been otherwise, his parents would hardly have forgotten his name at his brother's christening. The adult Ceausescu proceeded to compensate for this injury with all the means at his disposal: by erecting offices for himself in civic buildings, including museums and libraries. The requirement that all citizens were to hang a portrait of the dictator in their homes served the same purpose. Ceausescu hoped to make his presence felt by his ubiquitousness. Not for a moment was his existence to be ignored. Whatever he did, though, was too little to satisfy the child's natural, though previously repressed, needs—its need to be seen and recognized, to be acknowledged and taken seriously; its need for its name and its existence to never again be forgotten in the fundamental, damaging, and harmful way that it had been by his parents.

A mistreated child has no chance of maintaining this need at the level of consciousness. If the need remains unsatisfied, the child must repress it. As adults we can relieve that repression by no longer denying what happened to us, and we can attempt to satisfy this primal need in legitimate, nondestructive ways. We can also choose not to confront the truth of our childhood and, like Ceausescu and many like him, force others to satisfy the primal needs that have remained unconscious, even at the cost of their lives.

Ultimately, though, what was painfully lacking in childhood cannot be made good by repression and the fulfillment of substitute gratifications. Even when the acquisition of power fuels the illusion, allowing it to swell to staggering proportions, the number of victims will always be too small to sate the deadly, unconscious rage of the child that was prevented from living. The "victories" of Stalin, Hitler, and Ceausescu show that quite clearly. At the height of their power these men still feared their fathers' assaults, the mistreatment that fitted out their paranoid manias with its own private logic. Hitler had the places connected with his Austrian origins razed to the ground. By destroying the farms and villages of Rumania, Ceausescu sought to similarly "liquidate" his past. If the Rumanian people had not been able to free themselves of this monster, this process of liquidation would have seen no end.

Both the dictator and his wife were convinced that they were being the best of parents as they tortured "the people." This was the message they had learned from their parents early on, and they regarded it as absolutely binding. It can be seen in the last words uttered by Elena Ceausescu before her execution. As the soldiers attempted to tie her up, she shouted: "Children! Remember! I have been like a mother to you these last twenty years. Don't forget everything I have done for you!" During her trial Elena also swore that she had "sacrificed" herself for the people since the age of fourteen. Clearly, she was completely unconscious of the cynicism of such claims. She had learned to lend credibility to similar claims made by her parents and expected the same faith on the part of her "beloved people."

What did the Ceausescus' devoted "parental care" for their beloved victims consist of? To them, prohibiting abortion and contraceptives was a way of showing their affection. Only after a woman had reached the age of forty, and delivered the obligatory five children, was she allowed to have a legal abortion. In practice, that meant that a mother of seven children who was under forty would be refused treatment if she landed in a hospital, hemmorhaging after an illegal abortion, because the staff feared persecution. Such women were left to die a bloody death. The children were committed to an orphanage. Understandably, the orphanages of Rumania were full to overflowing, and it was from them that the dictator recruited future members of his "Securitate." But that wasn't all. The remaining children were sold in the West for adoption, and the hard currency so earned was spent on the luxuries with which the ruling family surrounded itself. How could children be used to make money in this way? one asks oneself. But the insanity did not stop there. The outlawing of abortion was justified as a means of raising the population to thirty million. Rumania, said the dictator, was to be a *great nation*. After all, a people blessed with a great leader should be great. In the face of such facts we react with understandable disbelief. We don't, however, react with incredulity when a grown-up hits and kicks a child, claiming: "I will teach you how to behave and one day you will thank me for it." That Ceausescu's drunken father, *the* ruler of the commonwealth of children, made such speeches, is beyond any doubt. Elena and Nicolae Ceausescu were deeply grateful to their parents for all the mistreatment they received. They expected the same gratitude from the people for their torture.

If the psychodynamics of child abuse were universally acknowledged today, a man like Nicolae Ceausescu could not succeed in plundering and humiliating an entire nation for twenty years in the guise of national salvation, with the goal of raising a whole nation as his applauding slaves. But his regime is a blueprint of the generally accepted tyranny imposed throughout the world with impunity on children in the name of "child rearing" and redemption "for your own good"—dispossession, exploitation, total control, torture, humiliation, disrespect, mistreatment, misuse, persecution, seduction, lies, terror, the deformation of the truth, and pitiless psychic cruelty. All carried out, thank you very much, with a smile and the promise of salvation.

The little girls, for instance, who were to cheer on the dictator at parades, had to stand shivering in their white shirts for many hours because the illustrious "father of the nation" believed that "effeminacy is bad for character." As part of the pedagogic vocabulary of our fathers, such a pronouncement would have been perfectly normal. Only today can one see how it glorifies heartless, sadistic chicanery.

It was well known that at the end of his regime Ceausescu had become a paranoiac. But no politician asked himself: How did he *become* paranoid? Only if one dares to ask this question does one get the answer that is so crucial for us all: How can we prevent madmen from gaining power over us?

Anyone who has the opportunity to study Ceausescu's childhood in more detail could easily come to see how his murderous, destructive rage, the rage that would later be disguised as promises of redemption, was produced. The TV reports that came out of Rumania gave us all an idea of the number of victims who again had to pay for our blindness in this respect.

Countless people with a personality structure similar to Hitler or Ceausescu inhabit our planet, destroying life wherever they can. We can and must make it impossible for such people to gain power over us in the future. And we could, if we chose, avail ourselves of the necessary knowledge to render such a thing impossible.

How can one recognize such people? Above all, by the way that they claim the enslavement of others to be their salvation and their own crimes to be actions taken in the best interests of others. When one keeps in mind the deceptive and manipulatory nature of the language of pedagogy, and knows what calamities can result, then one will be able to defend oneself against future tyrants. Without exception, such tyrants always use the language of traditional child rearing. And as long as people have not learned to see through the deceitfulness of such language and thereby recognize and reject it in the speeches of politicians of "national salvation," it will continue to serve them well. The notion that one mistreats a child and at the same time claims to be doing so for its own good was so axiomatic in the last generation that Stalinism in all its variant forms was able to gain an excellent place in the minds of many people. Fortunately the younger generation, who had been less exposed to violence and all kinds of cant, was able to reveal, reject, and dethrone such lies and prepare the way for true democracy.

Many well-known politicians and rulers, who are responsible for the fates of whole nations, met with Ceausescu. They received him with full honors, reached out the hand of political goodwill and even friendship. Not one seemed to notice that the person they were dealing with was the quintessence of vileness—

dissembling, smug snobbism, vacuousness and sheer destructiveness. Was that because these people stood to gain by collaborating with Ceausescu's elaborate lies and intrigues? That may be true of some of these politicians, though not for all. But the majority of them, unlike some younger politicians of today, were still the children of "poisonous pedagogy" (see *For Your Own Good*).

The thoughts of the man who spent his evenings watching films about Napoleon or thrillers were dominated, above all else, by the desire to turn himself into the "genius of the century"—if necessary, over the dead bodies of thousands of his countrymen. Concocting plans for this was part of Ceausescu's way of life. According to Pacepa, the head of "Securitate" until 1973, Ceausescu discussed these plans with him "in the garden, among the rose bushes," because he himself already went in fear of the bugging devices he had installed everywhere (see Ion Pacepa, Paris, 1987).

The report of a former "Securitate" man should perhaps be taken with a pinch of salt. But the things that the book *Horizons Rouges* reports have today, after the revolution, been by and large confirmed. Reading this book, one is barely able to believe that so many well-known politicians proved their absolute psychological illiteracy in connection with the unambiguously clear case of Ceausescu. We refuse to recognize these facts, or to believe them, because the lives of so many people are still entrusted to precisely these politicians.

We don't want to believe our own experience is true. Sadly, however, it *is* true. The children who died and continue to die in the hunger wards of Rumania confirm this fact. Their tortured faces also yield proof that the passionate defense of the right to life does not always flow with the milk of human kindness. Its origins are all too often hatred of the unwanted and unloved, from those who like Ceausescu were never really allowed to live as children and wish to inflict on other children the same state of lovelessness and unwantedness. Those children in the hunger wards have this hatred to thank for their existence. The question is, will they ever receive the necessary love for them not to later wish to take revenge for their own desperate fate on innocent people?

8

The Mistreated Child in the Lamentations of Jeremiah

IT REQUIRES A CONSIDERABLE ACT OF THE imagination for us to be able to conceive of the situation of a small child, totally exposed to the willfulness and, not infrequently, the madness of adults. This madness can quite readily coexist with a polished sociability on the part of the parents, so that it remains completely invisible. The fathers can be men invested with important positions, who enjoy universal respect, but who take out the repressed torture of their own childhoods on their children. The same is true of women. They may be regarded as excellent mothers, but remain completely blind to their children's needs because they learned as young girls that a child's needs do not count. As they never received protection, loving care, orientation, or tenderness from their own mothers, they had to suppress the accompanying needs. As a result, they remain blind to their own children's needs, unless positive experiences in their personal relationships have allowed this blindness to heal.

With reference to Eugene O'Neill's play *A Long Day's Journey into Night*, I described a mother who clung to the idealized image of her addictive father to such an extent that she had to pay the price for this self-deception not only with her own addiction, but with the destruction of her three sons (see *Banished Knowledge*, chapter 6). If we have had to survive a similar baptism by fire as children, we do not wish, as adults, to be reminded of it. We do not like having to empathize with an unhappy child, even if we were ourselves once that same child. Even if we do wish to do so, we run up against internal barriers, because as adults we have never had to experience the massive, inescapable defenselessness to which a child is frequently exposed. Nonetheless, we can find, in literature, art and in fairy tales, testimonies to the defenselessness of childhood—works created by adults, though they did not necessarily know, at a conscious level, what they were describing. In *Thou Shalt Not Be Aware*, I attempted to show how the truth about the mistreatment of children constantly finds expression. This happens, though, only with the help of symbols; the respective writer does not place his or her own repression in danger. What they cannot therefore know is that their repressed reality far exceeds their worst fantasies.

With reference to Kafka's novels and short stories, I attempted to show that it was in the realm of his unconscious that the truth about his early childhood found expression—a truth that, despite his critical stance toward his father, remained completely hidden to his conscious mind. *The Castle* tells us much about the situation of an unwanted and constantly deceived child; *The Trial* about the tortures of an unnamed, but ubiquitous guilt; *The Penal Colony* about the madness of punitive measures carried out against an unsuspecting child; *The Hunger Artist*, about the never-satisfied hunger for contact; *Metamorphosis*, about the state of mind of an unloved, misunderstood, and neglected child. The work of Gustave Flaubert, Samuel Beckett, and others shows how writers and poets are able to help to make the breakthrough to their truth, at least partially and in symbolic form, without concerning themselves with the realities behind those truths—that is, without finally taking full responsibility for what is shown. As a result, these testimonies to the truth do not ultimately help to wake people from their dangerous sleep.

Such testimonies are to be found not only in modern literature. The exercise of power by adults over defenseless children, frequently going as far as infanticide, and the disregard of the child's person, which is the experience in most (though hopefully not all) cultures, is reflected in the culture's literary works. In the Old Testament, for instance, we again come across the pattern that we know so well from our own experience of child rearing: punishment for disobedience, disloyalty, or the worshipping of other deities; the promise of reward and redemption for obedience; outbursts of rage and obsessional destructiveness. On the other side is the defenseless child. Because of its dependency on the adults around it, the child must humbly accept such bouts of rage. The reality of adult cruelty is so beyond its comprehension that the child is in a state of constant denial in order to survive.

Adults who have forgotten what in German can be called the "Ur-situation"—the defining context—of their existence, and who hold on to their repression, no longer remember how it was for that small child to live side by side with two omniscient, stern, and unpredictable parents. Many, however, are avid readers of the Bible. They also read the Bible to their children, demonstrating there confirmation that their method of child rearing is perfectly right. They themselves still wait for the redemption their parents once promised them. If it doesn't happen, they reason, then they have themselves to blame. They seek comfort in the Bible as it confirms them in their old hope that God—or their parents—will see to it that they are all right, even though reality contradicts them. They hope that the cruelty they had to endure is no more or less than the just punishment for their own wickedness. One can, after all, stop being bad. One can do many things to win God's love and acceptance—one can go to church, pray, practice charity. But the thought that one is at the mercy of a moody, unjust, and unpredictable God is unbearable. About that one can do nothing. The thought remains unfathomable, and one seeks a solution in illusion, in the belief that everything is really other than experience shows and proves it to be.

This is the situation in which many children find themselves. They try to help themselves by burdening themselves with guilt. They cling to the illusion that they must be able to do something to change their situation—the state of neglect, demeaning attacks, mistreatment, and deception in which they find themselves—if they would only try hard enough. And they do try. They try to forgive everything that they have had to endure so that at long, long last they might be loved and accepted. In the following passages I cite parts of the Lamentations of Jeremiah, written in the year 600 B.C. In them, the prophet rebels against cruelty in the manner of a vital, feeling, and seeing child. He constantly tries to seek comfort in the thought that torture is no more than the just and necessary punishment for his own misdemeanors:

FROM: REVISED STANDARD VERSION

Book I

12 Is it nothing to you, all you who pass by?
Look and see if there is any sorrow like my
sorrow

which was brought upon me,
which the Lord inflicted on the day of his
fierce anger.
13 *From on high he sent fire; into my bones he*
made it descend;
he spread a net for my feet; he turned me back;
he has left me stunned, faint all the day long.
14 *My transgressions were bound into a yoke;*
by his hand they were fastened together;
they were set upon my neck; he caused my
strength to fail;
the Lord gave me into the hands of those
whom I cannot withstand.
15 *The Lord flouted all my mighty men in the*
midst of me;
18 *The Lord is in the right, for I have*
rebelled against his word;
but hear, all you peoples, and behold my
suffering.
19 *I called to my lovers but they deceived me;*
20 *Behold, O Lord, for I am in distress, my soul*
is in tumult,
my heart is wrung within me, because I
have been very rebellious.
21 *Hear how I groan; there is none to comfort*
me.
All my enemies have heard of my trouble;
they are glad that thou has done it.
Bring thou the day thou hast announced,
and let them be as I am.
22 *Let all their evil doing come before thee;*
and deal with them
as thou has dealt with me
because of all my transgressions;
for my groans are many and my heart is
faint.

Book II

11 My eyes are spent with weeping; my soul is
in tumult.
17 The Lord has done what he purposed, has
carried out his threat;
as he ordained long ago, he has demolished
without pity.
18 Let tears stream down like a torrent day and
night!
Give yourself no rest, your eyes no respite!
19 Arise, cry out in the night, at the beginning
of the watches!
Pour out your heart like water before the
presence of the Lord!
Lift your hands to him for the lives of your
children,
who faint for hunger at the head of every
street.

Book III

1 I am the man who has seen affliction under
the rod of his wrath;
2 he has driven and brought me into darkness
without any light;
3 surely against me he turns his hand again
and again the whole day long.
6 He has made me dwell in darkness like the
dead of long ago.
7 He has walled me about so that I cannot
escape; he has put heavy chains on me;
8 though I call and cry for help, he shuts out
my prayer.
10 He is to me like a bear lying in wait, like a
lion in hiding.
11 He led me off my way and tore me to pieces;
he has made me desolate;

12 he bent his bow and set me as a mark for
his arrow.
14 I have become the laughingstock of all
peoples,
the burden of their songs all day long.
15 He has filled me with bitterness,
he has sated me with wormwood.
17 My soul is bereft of peace, I have forgotten
what happiness is;
19 Remember my affliction and my bitterness,
the wormwood and the gall!

This is more than a child can fathom; he desperately seeks consolation, finding it in his own apparent guilt, his own wickedness. This gives him hope:

20 My soul continually thinks of it and is
bowed down within me.
21 But this I call to mind, and therefore I have
hope:
22 The steadfast love of the Lord never ceases,
his mercies never come to an end;
23 they are new every morning; great is thy
faithfulness.
24 "The Lord is my portion," says my soul,
"therefore I will hope in him."
25 The Lord is good to those who wait for him,
to the soul that seeks him.
26 It is good that one should wait quietly.
27 It is good for a man that he bear the yoke in
his youth.
28 Let him sit alone in silence when he has
laid it on him;
29 let him put his mouth in the dust—there
may yet be hope;

30 let him give his cheek to the smiter, and be
filled with insults.
31 For the Lord will not cast off for ever,
32 but, though he cause grief, he will have
compassion
according to the abundance of
his steadfast love;
33 for he does not willingly afflict or grieve the
sons of men.
34 To crush under foot all the prisoners of the
earth,
35 to turn aside the right of a man in the
presence of the Most High,
36 to subvert a man in his cause, the Lord does
not approve.
37 Who has commanded and it came to pass,
unless the Lord has ordained it?
38 Is it not from the mouth of the Most High
that good and evil come?
39 Why should a living man complain,
a man, about the punishment of his sins?
40 Let us test and examine our ways, and
return to the Lord!
42 We have transgressed and rebelled, and
thou has not forgiven.
43 Thou has wrapped thyself with anger and
pursued as,
slaying without pity.

The feeling of outrage breaks through once again:

45 Thou has made us offscouring and refuse
among the peoples.
47 Panic and pitfall have come upon us,
devastation and destruction;

48 my eyes flow with rivers of tears because of the destruction.
49 My eyes will flow without ceasing, without respite,
50 until the Lord from heaven looks down and sees;
51 my eyes cause me grief.
52 I have been hunted like a bird by those who were my enemies without cause;
53 they flung me alive into the pit and cast stones on me;
54 water closed over my head; I said, "I am lost."
55 I called on thy name, O Lord, from the depths of the pit;
56 thou didst hear my plea, "Do not close thine ear to my cry for help!"
57 Thou didst come near when I called on thee;
thou didst say, "Do not fear!"
58 Thou hast taken up my cause, O Lord,
thou hast redeemed my life.
59 Thou has seen the wrong done to me, O Lord; judge thou my cause.
60 Thou hast seen all their vengeance,
all their devices against me.
64 Thou wilt requite them, O Lord,
according to the work of their hands.
65 Thou wilt give them dullness of heart;
thy curse will be on them.

Book V

19 But thou, O Lord, dost reign for ever;
thy throne endures to all generations.
20 Why dost thou forget us for ever,
why dost thou so long forsake us?

21 Restore us to thyself, O Lord, that we may
be restored!
22 Or hast thou utterly rejected us?
Art thou exceedingly angry with us?

After this desperate struggle against a clear consciousness of the injustice endured, after all attempts to convince oneself of the lie of one's own guilt, the simple truth once again asserts itself: "Art thou exceedingly angry with us?" With it comes the childlike wish: "Restore us to thyself, O Lord, that we may be restored!" A child who has been chastised, unlike a free child, cannot come back whenever it wishes. For that it needs the help of an adult.

The German commentary to this section of the Bible praises Jeremiah's trust, speaks of "God's love for the people that He chastises" and goes on: "This marvelous passage (verses 22–27) allows a tone of hope and faith to shine through in the midst of the darkness and lamentation. Even such pain cannot blind the prophet to God's fidelity." Such commentaries, which, in my opinion, have their origins in the spirit of "poisonous pedagogy," bury the truth of the lamentations. For it is not complaint that leads men into darkness, but pain, confusion, guilt, fear, and self-accusation. Were it to be heard and taken seriously, lamentation could bring light and clarity.

What finds unmistakable expression in the Lamentations of Jeremiah—albeit unconsciously and involuntarily—is the reality of a chastised, i.e., mistreated child. This child refuses to believe that the same parents who speak of love and loyalty are capable of a pitiless massacre—that *this* is what the truth is. Because it cannot believe what it sees without dying of the pain, the child gives credence to the opposite notion. It believes what is *said* and *promised*—that is, the word. It believes the opposite of what it has experienced.

Out of such a turning away from the facts, from righteous outrage at the truth, religions and ideologies have arisen and continue to arise. They promise people redemption from their sufferings and help them to deny their experience. In this way, for instance, Marxist-Leninism helped for decades to obscure the facts that perestroika has suddenly made abundantly clear. Without this view of the facts, nobody would be capable of changing them in any way.

It is for this reason that I have cited excerpts from the Lamentations. As I did with reference to Kafka's works, I wanted to let the mistreated child have his say and therefore omitted the historical allusions—in other words, the censorship of repression. I wanted to enable the reader to get close to the feelings of the tormented child, the child that has only one wish: that everything that he suffered *might not be true*. He may be wracked with pain, but the child still clings to the hope that the torture is no more than a response to his own guilt, that he is being chastised out of love. His own guilt is the mistreated child's only comfort!

The greater the panic-stricken fear of the repressed facts, of the return of the repressed, the more destructively and dangerously fanaticism rages. Whether it appears in religious or political form is not important; the one can easily turn into the other, as we can constantly witness today. What matters is the denial of crucial facts—and all orthodoxies have this characteristic in common. In the standard commentaries to Jeremiah one can discover an attitribute that still influences quite a few therapeutic methods. These therapists talk of the child's ambivalence toward its parents. They tell their patients to accept and learn to love both the good and the bad sides of their parents, who, they say, do always love their children despite everything. They insist that only when the child is in a position to do so, only when it can integrate both the good and the bad and learn "to love your parents' negative sides, too," can it "mature" and forgive.

Many therapists, in their efforts to relativize wickedness at all costs, recall the God of Creation, who punished Adam and Eve for learning to distinguish between good and evil, having eaten of the Tree of Knowledge. Already in those days it was less reprehensible to practice it than to see and unequivocally protest against evil. The fear of this deadly sin is also evident in the pronouncements and activities of many charitable organizations. The German Society for Child Protection, for instance, seeks to *understand* abusing parents but refuses to condemn the abuse. This organization is especially passionate about communicating this understanding for parents even if some of the real facts get forgotten along the way.

This, and similar therapeutic models, such as can also be found among family therapists, ignore the fact that the opposite is in fact true—that the child, just as Jeremiah expressed it twenty-six hundred years ago, goes on loving even the cruelest and most brutal of parents. Because it waits and hopes for salvation—for a miracle—it goes on clinging to them. The price of this illusion is the dangerous blindness that later allows adults to uphold the right to treat their children just as cruelly—for the precise reason that they have never called their toleration of their parents into question. But a person who is no longer a child and has the courage to mature by *wanting to see the truth* must be capable of *clearly and unequivocally* rejecting the cruelty he or she suffered. Only then will he or she refuse to contribute to the success of evil. This realization apparently unnerves both psychoanalysts and family therapists, system theorists, and many social workers because it calls their parents' actions into question. Jeremiah's consolation, however, cannot be ours. If we maintain this attitude of unending tolerance for God or our parents, we are in danger of delivering ourselves into the hands of people who *promise* us salvation and healing while remaining blind to what they really *do*.

The redemption we hope for will evade us so long as we cause self-damnation in our children and do not learn to avoid this. Unfortunately, children today are still punished and made to feel guilty about their natural, healthy impulses and reactions—sometimes with the rejoinder that this is God's will. Any child who has, in its early years, been overloaded with fears and pains that have not been physiologically caused, has been driven into the damnation of guilt-fear. Its feelings reflect what it has been taught: "If such things are inflicted on me, it must be my fault. There must be something wrong with me. *I* am the cause of my sufferings."

There are children who have been subjected to unnecessary medico-technical operations and check-ups in the first years of their lives. This is, among other things, frequently the result of doctors not taking seriously the real causes of the child's symptoms. Instead, they place their faith in all kinds of technical apparatus. Such children find themselves without consolation and abandoned in their isolation because their parents have faith only in the marvels of technology. These children will remain damned and continue to live in fear of the unknown until they can clarify such confusion in a deep-going therapy. Their "salvation" will come with the progressive relief of the traumatic elements.

PART THREE

Giving Up Hypocrisy

9

The Liberating Experience of Painful Truth

THE MISTREATED AND NEGLECTED CHILD IS completely alone in the darkness of confusion and fear. Surrounded by arrogance and hatred, robbed of its rights and its speech, deceived in its love and its trust, disregarded, humiliated, mocked in its pain, such a child is blind, lost, and pitilessly exposed to the power of ignorant adults. It is without orientation and completely defenseless.

Its whole being would like to shout out its anger, give voice to its feeling of outrage, call for help. But that is exactly what it may not do. All its normal reactions, the reactions with which nature has endowed it to help it survive, remain blocked. If no witness comes to its aid, these natural reactions would enlarge and prolong the child's sufferings. Ultimately, the child could die of them.

Thus, the healthy impulse to protest against inhumanity has to be suppressed. The child attempts to extinguish and erase from memory everything that has happened to it, in order to banish from consciousness the burning outrage, fury, fear, and the unbearable pain—as it hopes, forever. What remains is a feeling of its own guilt, rather than outrage that it is forced to kiss the hand that beats it and beg for forgiveness—something that unfortunately happens more than one imagines.

The abused child goes on living within those who have survived such torture, a torture that ended with total *repression. They* live with the darkness of fear, oppression, and threats. When all its attempts to move the adult to heed its story have failed, it resorts to the language of symptoms to make itself heard. Enter addiction, psychosis, criminality.

If, as adults, we nevertheless begin to have an inkling of why we are suffering and ask a specialist whether these sufferings could have a connection with our childhood, we will usually be told that this is very unlikely to be the case. And if it were, that we should learn forgiveness. It is the resentment at the past, we are told, that is making us ill.

In those by-now familiar groups in which addicts and their relations go into therapy together, the following belief is invariably expressed. Only when you have forgiven your parents for everything they did to you can you get well. Even if both parents were alcoholics, even if they mistreated, confused, exploited, beat, and totally overloaded you, you must forgive them everything. Otherwise, your illness will not be cured. There are many programs going by the name of "therapy," whose basis consists of first learning to express one's feelings in order to see what happened in childhood. Then, however, comes "the work of forgiveness," which is apparently necessary if one is to heal. Many young people who have AIDS or are drug-addicted die in the wake of their effort to forgive so much. What they do not realize is that they are trying to keep the repression of their childhood intact.

Some therapists fear this truth. They work under the influence of various interpretations culled from both Western and Oriental religions, which preach forgiveness to the once-mistreated child. Thereby, they create a new vicious circle for people who, from their earliest years, have been caught in the vicious circle of pedagogy. This, they refer to as "therapy." In so doing, they lead them into a trap from which there is no escape, the same trap that once rendered their natural protests impossible, thus causing the illness in the first place. Because such therapists, caught as they are in the pedagogic system, cannot help patients to resolve the consequences of the traumatization they have suffered, they offer them traditional morality instead.

In recent years I have been sent many books from the United States of America describing different kinds of therapeutic intervention by authors with whom I am not familiar. Many of these authors presume that forgiveness is an indispensable condition for successful therapy. This notion appears to be so widespread in therapeutic circles that it is not always called into question—something urgently needed. For forgiveness does not resolve latent hatred and self-hatred but can cover them up in a very dangerous way.

I know of the case of one woman, whose mother was sexually abused as a child by both her father and brother. Reared in a convent, this woman learned "the blessing of forgiveness" by heart. She continued to worship her father and brother without the slightest trace of bitterness. While her daughter was still an infant, she frequently left the child "in the care of" her thirteen-year-old nephew, while she went blithely off to the movies with her husband. While she was gone, the pubescent babysitter indulged his sexual desires on the body of her baby daughter. When the daughter later sought help in psychoanalytic counseling, the analyst told her she should on no account blame her mother. Her intentions had not been bad, she was told. She had had no idea that her babysitter was routinely abusing her child. The mother, it seems, was literally clueless. When the child began to develop dietary disturbances, she anxiously consulted a number of doctors. They assured her that the disturbances in her eating habits came from "teething." Thus, the gears of this forgiveness-machine were functioning almost perfectly—and, at the expense of the truth and the lives of all concerned. Fortunately, they don't always function as well.

In her highly creative, remarkable book *The Obsidian Mirror: An Adult Healing from Incest* (Seal Press, 1988), Louise Wisechild describes how she succeeded in deciphering her body's messages and communications, and thereby her feelings, so that she was gradually able to free her childhood from repression. This took place in a successful therapy involving bodywork and written accounts of her experiences. Gradually, she discovered in detail what she had totally banished from consciousness: that she had been sexually molested by her grandfather at the age of four; that she was subsequently abused by an uncle and finally also by her stepfather. A woman therapist was willing and brave enough to work with her on this horrific journey of self-discovery, in spite of the manifest torture to which the patient had been subjected. Nevertheless, even in this most successful therapy Louise sometimes felt that she should forgive her mother. On the other hand, she strongly felt that this might be wrong. Fortunately, the therapist didn't insist too much on this point. She gave Louise the freedom to follow her own feelings and to discover that it was not forgiveness that made her strong in the end. Helping the patient to resolve the guilt feelings that had been imposed upon her—the ultimate purpose, presumably, of therapy—doesn't mean to burden her with an additional demand, a demand that could only serve to cement those feelings of guilt. A quasi-religious act of forgiveness can never resolve patterns of self-destruction.

Why should this woman, after showing her concern for her mother for thirty years, forgive her crime, when that mother had never made the slightest effort to see what she had done to her daughter? On one occasion, as the child, rigid with fear and disgust, was forced to lie under the heavy, male body of her uncle, she caught sight of her mother in the mirror as she approached the door. The child hoped to be saved, but the mother turned and disappeared. When Louise was an adult, she heard her mother say that she could only cope with her fear of that uncle if her children were around her. When the daughter tried to discuss her rape at the hands of her stepfather, her mother wrote her that she never wished to see her again. Even in many such blatant cases, the pressure to forgive, which effectively prevents the chance of a successful therapy, is hardly seen as the absurd demand that it is. It is just this common pressure to forgive that mobilizes old fears in the patient that oblige him or her to believe such an authority. What can it possibly achieve, except a quiet conscience for the therapist?*

In many cases much can be destroyed with a single, fundamentally wrong, confusing sentence. That it is well anchored in tradition and has been implanted in us since our earliest childhood only makes matters worse. What is involved here is an outrageous misuse of power, by which therapists are wont to ward off their powerlessness and fear. Patients, for their part, are convinced

*I have slightly revised the last two paragraphs for this revised edition after reviewing a letter from Louise Wisechild, who provided me with more specific information about her own view of her therapy.

that the therapist holds this view as a result of the incontrovertible evidence of experience and so believe this "authority." They cannot know—and it is almost impossible for them to discover—that what this claim in fact discloses is the therapist's own fear of the mistreatment suffered at the hands of his or her parents. How are patients meant to resolve their feelings of guilt under such circumstances? On the contrary, they will simply be confirmed.

Preaching forgiveness reveals the pedagogic nature of some therapies. In addition, it exposes the powerlessness of the preachers. In a sense, it is odd that they call themselves "therapists" at all. "Priests" would be more apt. What ultimately emerges is the continuation of the blindness inherited in childhood, the blindness that a real therapy could relieve. What is constantly repeated to patients—until they believe it, and the therapist is mollified—is: "Your hate is making you ill. You must forgive and forget. Then you will be well." But it was not hatred that drove patients to mute desperation in their childhood, by alienating them from their feelings and their needs. It was such morality with which they were constantly pressured.

It was my experience that it was precisely the opposite of forgiveness—namely, rebellion against mistreatment suffered, the recognition and condemnation of my parents' misleading opinions and actions, and the articulation of my own needs—that ultimately freed me from the past. In my childhood, these things had been ignored in the name of "a good upbringing," and I myself learned to ignore them for decades in order to be the "good" and "tolerant" child my parents wished me to be. But today I know: I always needed to expose and fight against opinions and attitudes that I considered destructive of life wherever I encountered them, and not to tolerate them. But I could only do this effectively once

I had felt and experienced what was inflicted on me earlier. By preventing me from feeling the pain, the moral-religious injunction to forgive did nothing but hinder this process.

The demand for good behavior has nothing to do with either an effective therapy or life. For many people in search of help, it closes the path to freedom. Therapists allow themselves to be led by their own fear—the mistreated child's fear of its parents' revenge—and by the hope that good behavior might one day be able to buy the love their parents denied them. The price that patients have to pay for this illusory hope is high indeed. Given false information, they cannot find the path to self-fulfillment.

By refusing to forgive, I give up my illusions. A mistreated child, of course, cannot live without them. But a grown-up therapist must be able to manage it. His or her patients should be able to ask: "Why should I forgive, when no one is asking me to? I mean, my parents refuse to understand and to know what they did to me. So why should I go on trying to understand and forgive my parents and whatever happened in their childhood, with things like psychoanalysis and transactional analysis? What's the use? Whom does it help? It doesn't help my parents to see the truth. But it does prevent me from experiencing my feelings, the feelings that would give me access to the truth. But under the bell-jar of forgiveness, feelings cannot and may not blossom freely." Such reflections are, unfortunately, not common in therapeutic circles, in which forgiveness is the ultimate law. The only compromise that is made consists of differentiating between false and correct forms of forgiveness. But therapy requires only the "correct" form. And this goal may never be questioned.

I have asked many therapists why it is that they believe their patients must forgive if they are to become well, but I have never received a halfway acceptable answer. Clearly, they had never questioned their assertion. It was, for them, as self-evident as the mistreatment with which they grew up. I cannot conceive of a society in which children are not mistreated, but respected and lovingly cared for, that would develop an ideology of forgiveness for incomprehensible cruelties. This ideology is indivisible with the command "Thou shalt not be aware" and with the repetition of that cruelty on the next generation. It is our children who pay the price for our lack of awareness. Our fear of our parents' revenge is the basis of our morality.

However, by means of gradual therapeutic disclosure that dispenses with bogus morality and pedagogy, this misleading ideology can be stopped. Survivors of mistreatment need to discover their own truth if they are to free themselves of its consequences. Moralizing leads them away from this truth.

An effective therapy cannot be achieved if the mechanisms of pedagogy continue to operate. It requires recognition of the damage caused by our upbringing, whose consequences it should resolve. It must make patients' feelings available to them—and accessible for the entirety of their lives. This can help them to orientate and be at one with themselves. Moralizing appeals can result in barring access to this self-knowledge.

A child can excuse its parents, if they in their turn are prepared to recognize and admit to their failures. But the demand for forgiveness that I often encounter can pose a danger for therapy, even though it is an expression of our culture. Mistreatment of children is the order of the day, and those errors are *therefore* trivialized by the majority of adults. Forgiving can have negative consequences, not only for the individual, but for society at large, because it can mean disguising erroneous opinions and attitudes, and involves drawing a curtain across reality so that we cannot see what is taking place behind it.

The possibility of change depends on whether there is a sufficient number of enlightened witnesses to create a safety net for the growing consciousness of those who have been mistreated as children, so that they do not fall into the darkness of forgetfulness, from which they will later emerge as criminals or the mentally ill. Cradled in the "net" provided by such enlightened witnesses, these children can grow to be conscious adults, adults who live *with* and not against their past and who will *therefore* be able to do everything they can to create a more humane future for us all.

It has already been scientifically proved that weeping caused by sadness, pain, and fear not only causes tears to fall. Stress hormones, which lead to a general relaxation of the body, are also released. Of course, this cannot be equated with therapy. Nevertheless, it is an important discovery that should find its way into the treatments used by therapeutic practitioners. So far, though, the opposite has been the case. Patients are given tranquilizers to calm them. What would happen if they began to gain access to the causes of their symptoms! The problem with medical pedagogy is that the majority of those involved, the institutions and specialists, in no way wish to know *why* it is people become ill. The result of this denial is that countless chronically ill people become permanent residents of our prisons and clinics, while billions are spent by the government on keeping mum about the truth. Those affected must on no account realize that they can be helped to understand the language of their childhood, thereby truly reducing their suffering or even relieving it altogether.

If we had the courage to confront the facts about the repression of childhood mistreatment and its consequences, this would be possible. One look at the specialist literature on the subject, however, shows just how lacking such courage is. By contrast, the literature is full of appeals to our good intentions, all kinds of noncommittal and unverifiable advice, and, above all, moral preaching. Everything, all cruelty endured in childhood, is to be forgiven. If that doesn't do the trick, then the state must pay for the lifelong care and treatment of invalids and the chronically ill. But with the help of the truth, they could be cured.

It has now been proved that though repression may be crucial for a child, it should not necessarily be the fate of adults. A small child's dependency on its parents, its trust in them, its longing to love and be loved, are limitless. To exploit this dependency, to deceive a child in its longing, confuse it, and then proceed to sell this as "child rearing" is a criminal act—a criminal act committed hourly and daily out of ignorance, indifference, and the refusal to give up such behavior. The fact that the majority of such crimes are committed unconsciously does not, unfortunately, allay the calamitous consequences. The abused child's body will register the truth, while its consciousness refuses to acknowledge it. By repressing the pain and the accompanying situations, the infantile organism averts death—its fate, were it to consciously experience such traumatization.

What remains is the vicious circle of repression: the true story, which has been suppressed in the body, produces symptoms so that it could at last be recognized and taken seriously. But our consciousness refuses to comply, just as it did in childhood—because it was *then* that it learned the life-saving function of repression, and because no one has subsequently explained that as grown-ups we are not condemned to die of our knowledge, that, on the contrary, such knowledge would help us in our quest for health.

The dangerous teaching of "poisonous pedagogy"—

"Thou Shalt Not Be Aware Of What Was Done To You"—reappears in the methods of treatment practiced by doctors, psychiatrists, and therapists. With medication and mystifying theories they try to influence their patients' memories as deeply as possible, in order that they never find the cause of their illness. These lie, almost without exception, in the psychic and physical mistreatment and neglect suffered in childhood.

Today, we know that AIDS and cancer involve a drastic collapse of the body's immune system, and that this physical "resignation" precedes the sick person's loss of hope. Incredibly, hardly anyone has taken the step that these discoveries suggest: that we can regain our hope, if our distress signals are finally heard. If our repressed, hidden story is at last perceived with full consciousness, even our immune system can regenerate itself. But who is there to help, when all the "helpers" fear their own personal history? And so we play the game of blindman's buff with each other—patients, doctors, medical authorities—because until now only a few people have experienced the fact that emotional access to the truth is the *indispensable precondition* of healing. In the long run, we can only function with consciousness of the truth. This also holds for our physical well-being. Bogus traditional morality, destructive religious interpretations, and confusion in our methods of child rearing all make this experience harder and hinder our initiative. Without a doubt, the pharmaceutical industry also profits from our blindness and despondency. However, each of us has been given only one life and only one body. It refuses to be fooled, insisting with all means at its disposal that we do not deceive it.

If, one day, the secret of childhood were to become no longer a secret, the state would be able to save the immense sums that it spends on hospitals, psychiatric clinics, and prisons maintaining our blindness. That this might deliberately happen is almost too incredible a thought. The money could be spent helping people relieve the repression that makes them ill, to help them recognize what happened to them in childhood and to resolve its consequences, so that they might live a responsible, conscious life. People who *know and feel* what happened to them in their childhood will never want to harm others. They will protect life and not wish to destroy it, for that is our biological purpose.

Sadly, there is little to be proud of in our tradition of child torture and child murder. It is to be thanked for our cynicism and indifference to the suffering of children. Using different examples, this is what I have tried to show in this book—that tradition is also to be thanked for our blindness to the fact that we are in the process of destroying the generations to come, and, ultimately, life itself, with our cruelty sanctioned by tradition. It is therefore high time that we were brave enough to orient ourselves to the facts and to our own experience, rejecting that destructive inheritance, even though it may have, up to now, appeared in the best of lights.

10

Protecting Life After Birth

DESPITE THE MANY GLIMMERS OF TRUTH THAT 1989 brought to us, the same year was seen out in Germany with an unexpected, and unsettling, event. In numerous Catholic churches, the bells were rung for fifteen minutes to proclaim to the faithful that abortion was a sin. In the midst of the euphoria at the tearing down of the Berlin Wall and the growing consciousness among young people, we were thrown back into the Middle Ages—an era in which much of what we know today was as yet undiscovered, and which, anyway, had little interest in enlightenment. Church bells have never been rung to proclaim the mistreatment of children sinful. They weren't rung as Hitler organized the mass deportation of Jews throughout Europe, or as Stalin presided over the extermination of millions. And they didn't ring as Ceausescu terrorized his nation, using its children as apprentice "Securitate" men, who would later open fire on real children. But now they did ring, for a full fifteen minutes, so *that even more unwanted and later tortured children could be born into the world*!

In disbelief, one asks oneself: Is it possible that the

people behind such actions really are so clueless? Do they not know that no less than one hundred percent of all seriously abused children are unwanted? Do they not know what that can lead to? Do they not know that mistreatment is a parent's way of taking revenge on the children they never wanted? Shouldn't the authorities do everything in their power, in the light of this information, to see to it that the only children who are born are wanted, planned for, and loved? If they did, then we could put an end to the creation and continuation of evil in our world. To force the role of a mother on a woman who does not wish to be a mother is an offense not just against her, but against the whole human community, because the child she brings into the world is likely to take criminal revenge for its birth, as do the many (mis)leaders threatening our lives. All wars we ever had were the deeds of once unwanted, heinously mistreated children. It is the right to *lived* life that we must protect wherever and whenever it is threatened. And it should never be sacrificed to an abstract idea.

Not everyone is capable of thinking in real, concrete terms. Many seek refuge in religious beliefs. In their weakness, they place their trust in "relics," awaiting salvation at the hands of one stronger than themselves. Anyone who claims to be a strong and knowledgeable authority for such people, and to be acting on their behalf, has the duty to be conscious of the appropriate facts. If they aren't, if they ignore or neglect that duty, claiming instead that their palpable lack of information and their abstract conceptions of "life" are sanctioned by God and practiced in the name of humanity, they are acting *against* life, by misusing the weakness and trust of the faithful and dangerously confusing them. The injunction against abortion goes even further: Consciously or unconsciously, it represents support for cruelty against children and active complicity in the creation of unwanted existences, existences that can easily become a liability for the community at large.

When I see the passion with which Catholic priests—men childless by choice—fight against abortion, I can't help asking what it is that motivates them. Is it a desire to prove that unlived life, as perhaps their own destinies suggest, is more important and more valuable than lived life? Was that, perhaps, how the parents of those passionately committed to stopping abortion thought, though they expressed it in different ways? Or is it a case of seeing to it that others share the same fate as oneself? Both are possible. Both are dangerous, when people are driven to blind and destructive actions by the dead hand of their own repression.

It is, in fact, not surprising to find that those who are both victims and apologists for the use of violence and severity against children are often those who most passionately proclaim their love of the unborn child, i.e., the kernel of life. Abortion can, indeed, be seen as the most powerful symbol of the psychic annihilation and mutilation practiced since time immemorial on children. But to combat this evil merely at the symbolic level deflects us from the reality we should not evade for a moment longer: the reality of the abused and humiliated child, which, as a result of its disavowed and unresolved injuries, will insidiously become, either openly or aided by hypocrisy, a danger to society.

It is above all the children already born that have a right to life—a right to coexistence with adults in a world in which, with or without the help of the church, violence against children has been unequivocally outlawed. Until such legislation exists, talk of "the right to life" remains not only a mockery of humanity but a contribution to its destruction.

Few countries in Europe have, in fact, made parental

violence against children a criminal act. Sweden, Norway, Finland, Denmark, and, recently, Austria have done so. The largest European countries, however—France, Great Britain, and Germany—still refuse to enact such legislation. Their argument against it employs the familiar language of pedagogy. It is, they say, "in the interests of the child" *not* to have such laws. It is even claimed that the mistreatment of children would increase if parents were to be threatened with prosecution. In *Banished Knowledge*, I analyzed in detail the motives and reasons behind such arguments in connection with the writings of a number of "professional helpers," so I will not go into it again here. Suffice it to say that ten years' experience in Sweden has proved precisely the opposite. The law against corporal punishment, introduced ten years ago in Sweden, has set in motion an irreversible process that sets that country apart from its European neighbors. Thanks to that legislation, the fact that the physical maltreatment of children is a manifestly criminal act has now become anchored in the consciousness of the Swedish people. Which is not to say that criminality has been abolished overnight as a result of such legislation. It does mean, however, that only a small minority of the population, through their ignorance, furthers the cause of criminality. There is, for instance, a religious sect in Sweden that counsels the use of physical force against children with recourse to biblical precedent. But in the society at large such views win few friends. In the eyes of the aware majority, such a sect is merely a destructive fringe element.

In the most powerful European countries, however, the situation is quite different. There, only a minority is committed to the abolition of child abuse. The majority, drawing on a long tradition, rests comfortably in the conviction that the use of force is the best way of rearing children. Peter Newell, founder of the organization

EPPOCH, has reported in his book *Children Are People, Too* (London, 1989) that since legislation was introduced in Sweden only one case—involving a father, and punished with a small fine—has come before the courts. And though such information needs to be supplemented by other data, it nonetheless appears perfectly logical that a criminal act is committed less often when it is made illegal than when it is permitted. Why, then, do the powers-that-be go on ignoring this self-evident logic, two hundred years after the declaration of human rights? Why is it still not illegal to hit a defenseless child when it is an indictable offense to strike a grown-up—someone who can, after all, defend him- or herself? How many arguments must still be mustered before this inhuman practice is finally, and unequivocally, outlawed?

Even if most civic authorities do not know—or do not wish to know—that their refusal to pass such legislation only contributes to the growth of crime, terrorism, drug addiction, widespread psychic illness, and the survival of ignorance, they surely have to recognize the indisputable fact that children are people and have the right not to be beaten, as do we all. It is to be assumed, therefore, that Peter Newell's initiative to change the laws governing the mistreatment of children in England will spread to France and Germany, thereby putting an end to ignorance of and complicity in this, the gravest of crimes against humanity.

I agree with Peter Newell's view that such legislative reform would be of epochal significance. At last, victims of mistreatment would be freed from their acute, and paralyzing, guilt-fears—feelings that later prompt them to be in their turn the persecutors of others. By categorically condemning the criminal actions of past generations, such laws would also enlighten the coming generation and help it to avoid the blind repetition of its forefathers' guilt. It would also bring an immediate change to the way that parents behave.

Only then, when the law has unequivocally condemned the mistreatment of children as a criminal offense—making it punishable, say, with a fine—can a change in public awareness be expected. Criminality may not disappear in a trice, as a result. But such legislation will at least fill all those gaps in our consciousness that allow us to go on referring to such crimes as "socialization" or "upbringing." It would set an important caesura, marking the beginning of a process leading to a real humanity, a humanity that would create the necessary conditions for fundamental change to our way of living.

The horror of Hitler and Stalin, and the way in which their deeds and ideologies spread across the continent of Europe like a grotesque plague when I was young, taught me what price human beings pay—or make others pay—for their blindness. It also taught me that this blindness cannot be allowed to continue. Young people can today learn the same lessons from Ceausescu's example and others—above all, that dictators, once they have established themselves, can, with the help of the technical means available to them today, hold on to power far longer than they could before and are more difficult to topple without the loss of many lives. Only under the favorable conditions created by Gorbachev's courage to face the facts did the Rumanian people manage to free themselves from the maniacal and destructive political machine one madman, attempting—and failing—to save himself from the fears rooted in his childhood, had created.

One of today's tasks is to take preventive measures and thereby see to it that our children's future is not left to chance. That can only happen if we attempt to understand and avoid the origins of the kind of situation that the Rumanian people were forced to endure for twenty years. And we must do everything we can to prevent similar situations occurring. *In the light of our knowledge today, they do not need to occur.* Once the wall of silence surrounding childhood has been completely demolished, once people have access to the information they need—from the press, from books dealing with the subject, or in their own experiences in therapy—to explain how fantasies of revenge and the hunger for revenge arise, and once legislation outlawing the mistreatment of children has been passed, we will stop helping ignorance breed destructiveness and crime.

Then it will finally be visible to the great majority of people that a human being comes into the world as a highly sensitive creature, and that, from the first day of its life, it learns the nature of good and evil—learning faster, and more effectively, than it ever will again. Only then will we realize with horror, what these tiny, immensely sensitive creatures did learn, and learn indelibly, as they were treated like so much inert matter that their parents—our forefathers—sought to mold into malleable objects. Hammering at this creature as they would at a piece of metal, they finally got the obedient robot they wanted. In the process, they fashioned tyrants and criminals. The products of this process—those who managed to come through with a small part of their potential intact—spent the rest of their lives claiming that the mistreatment they were subjected to as children had not harmed them one bit. And how could it be otherwise, if they did not know how mutilated they had been? Many still don't know, don't know that they forfeited a wealth of possibilities as their souls—and that means also their capacity to perceive—were mutilated. Only their children's children, who grew up with more freedom, will realize this in all its implications. Thanks to their consciousness and knowledge of such crimes in the past, they will be able to avoid them in the future. They will, I am sure, also do everything they can to counter blindness with enlightenment, knowing that it is just this blindness that enables ignorant and irresponsible people to climb to the pinnacles of power.

Afterword to the Paperback Edition: Recovery from Self-Betrayal*

THROUGHOUT TIME, PEOPLE IN DISTRESS HAVE been seeking help from others: from sages, priests, gurus, psychologists and groups of different kinds. They have never known that, for the most part, out of all these people, none could lend real assistance because they too, like most other human beings, fear the only truth that can really help. That truth is about the origins of human suffering: the repressed tragic experiences of our childhood. The repression of injuries endured in a childhood is the hidden cause of our later suffering.

For the child, this repression was necessary because otherwise he would have died from the overwhelming pain. However, adults need not die if they decide to become conscious. They can set themselves free from their symptoms and, at long last, be happy in themselves and in their lives as soon as they acknowledge the old wounds and let them heal. This becomes possible

*This essay first appeared (in slightly different form) in the critical analysis of AA programs by Ken Ragge, *More Revealed* (Alere Publishing, 1992).

when we feel the strong emotions we had to repress in childhood in order to survive, when we take them seriously, clarify their meaning and learn that our pain and rage are justified. This happens when we condemn the abuse without so-called moral objections and find our genuine, authentic needs. Anything else we may do, however well rooted in our culture and tradition, is betrayal and self-betrayal as long as it is based on the denial of truth and on the ignorance of real, provable knowledge.

What do we do if suddenly we hear unusual noises in our car? Or if we even suspect it is not running well? We take it to a skilled mechanic to find out what is wrong. We expect him to check the car and to find out why it is not running well before he proceeds to repair it. We would not entrust our car to a person uninterested in finding the cause of the problem or to one who would stubbornly dispute its importance. We would probably easily recognize that such a mechanic would make matters even worse.

But what we do for our car we are very often unable to do for ourselves. We often deliver up our souls without hesitation to exactly this kind of "expert." Why? Why are we able to take account of the skill of a person before we entrust him with our car but not with someone we decide to entrust with our soul? Is it because we learned from our parents early in our lives to ignore the existence of our soul—its laws, its plight, its despair and its needs? Is it because we learned not to care, not to feel the endured humiliations, not to know our rights, and not to ask questions? Is it because we are unaware of our own life history and don't want to know it for we are too afraid of feeling old pain? Or is it simply because we do not know how to feel this pain or that we can feel it safely? All these reasons, together, probably give the explanation. People abused and betrayed in childhood—and there are few who were not at the very least betrayed by "poisonous pedagogy"*—are not free to see through manipulation unless they lose their blindness in an effective therapy; they accept absurdities without resistance because that is what they are used to. Until recently, nobody actually knew how we could bring our forgotten (but stored up in our body and still very active) life history to light and, in this light, alleviate our pain. This concept has nothing to do with Freud and his followers. It is a new discovery, not yet taught in universities.

What would we do if we were hit by a reckless driver and left with a broken leg? We would have a doctor treat the injury as soon as possible so that it could heal properly. We would not go to a priest who would ask us to pray, or to an exorcist to cast out demons. Nor would we go to other people with broken bones who would treat our predicament as bad behavior and advise us how to behave, who would lead us to believe that everything we have to do is to forget the pain and the broken bones and forgive the driver. At least where our bones are concerned, we would regard such demands as unreasonable and bizarre.

But again, not if it is a question of our soul. When our heart and our soul are broken we often go to ignorant and blind people who may even go so far as to ridicule our invisible but very real fracture. We go to people who cannot or do not want to understand because they are so terribly frightened of their own pain, pain over which they fear being misunderstood or ridiculed. They sometimes call themselves therapists but don't realize they are trying to escape from their own painful history if possible, to "cure" themselves at our cost. They treat us according to the principles they themselves learned from their own childhood treatment: "You must behave and remain

*See Alice Miller, *For Your Own Good* (Farrar, Straus and Giroux, 1983).

lifeless, exactly as I was forced to do, you too must give up your feelings, your truth." We also go to people who pretend to be the highest authority in "recovery" today, but who use, uncritically, the poisonous pedagogy: "We understand your anger with the driver, we even encourage you to feel it, but only for a while. Then you have to pull yourself together, let your feelings go, exercise 'detachment' and 'positive thinking' and, above all, you must forgive or else your bones will never heal." "Why not?" we should be able to ask. "Isn't the recovery process dependent on the truth of the feelings and needs stored in our body? Don't our feelings and needs reveal important messages? Why do you want to take them away from us? Don't you realize how destructive your so-called 'moral' chatter is?"

Even though this "morality" is well rooted in our traditions and religions, killing one's feelings is contrary to Nature. Animals kill their young if they are sick and too weak to survive, but the healthy ones enjoy care and protection so they can live. Only the human child is condemned to an existence between life and death. It is no wonder so many people, looking for a means to escape this horror, end up addicted: to alcohol, to drugs, to overeating or to attending daily group meetings and being indoctrinated. But an addiction is not a safe refuge and, above all, it is no longer necessary. A different, healthy way to get rid of the horror has been found: to face it, to feel it, and to resolve its consequences. Even for those who have always tried to escape from their wounds because this seemed to be the one and only healthy way out, today, for the first time in our history, there is another option. We can make a choice. We can save our lives when we are prepared to search out our truth and when we refuse to be intimidated by the ridicule and ignorance of others. Now there are methods that enable us to access our life history, not with hypnosis, but by giving us leadership, autonomy and responsibility.

These methods have been very carefully developed by different therapists.

What you are going to find has always been within you. It has given you considerable anguish but only because it was denied, avoided and feared. Once you can face it, it will help you, it will guide you. You will recognize your fear as what it really is. Perhaps it is simply the fear of the child who is afraid of punishment if he acknowledges and speaks the truth. But you will not be punished now. Now, as an adult, you can insist on your right to feel your reality. You no longer need to cling to the empty word *spirituality*, a word that soon becomes meaningless because it is used for everything and says nothing that can't be said without using it. Your real, felt feelings will never kill you; they will help you find direction. Only the unfelt yet powerful emotions and needs, the feared and banished ones, can kill us.

Researchers are now beginning to grasp the truth that cancer can often be the last available, the ultimate, language of these repressed feelings. Therapists were surprised to see that once patients could feel, could express themselves, could take their unwanted emotions seriously and develop them into a direct and healthy language, full recovery was possible.*

To properly heal a broken bone you must consult a doctor. But the specific causes of your suffering can only be found by yourself. With the right assitance you can find them. When you are on the path toward your unique, unmistakable life history, you are mending your "fractures." Only one person can fully understand and heal them: you. The better you learn to take your feelings seriously and to understand them in depth, the quicker you will see through lies, humiliations and manipulations, and the more strongly you will be able to resist them.

*See Lydia Temoshok and Henry Dreher, *The Type C Connection* (Random House, 1992; Plume, 1993).

What is addiction really? It is a sign, a signal, a symptom of distress. It is a language that tells us about a plight that must be understood. The drug business would not flourish if there were not so many people who, in refusing to acknowledge their wounds, are in a permanent state of self-betrayal. Thus, people work to get rid of symptoms instead of searching out the cause.

There are plenty of means to combat symptoms of distress: medication, sermons, numerous "treatments," "miracles," threats, cults, pedagogical indoctrination and even blackmail. They can all work for a while, but only because they reinforce the repression and reinforce the fear of resolving it. However, many people who become abstinent this way are driven into another addiction because the real reasons for becoming addicted must be kept hidden. A lot of money and fame comes from this business of repression because it satisfies the longings of so many grown-up children: to be loved as a good child (I am blind as you want me to be. I am ready to forget all your cruelty, even at the cost of my life. Can you love me now?). In the long term, we have to pay a high price for this repression. The repressed story continues to try, again and again, to be heard at long last. Thus, your plight will look for other symptoms, another language, until it is taken seriously enough. An addiction is an attempt by a person in despair, who is not allowed to be in despair, to get rid of his or her memory, to forget his or her plight. Of course, this "solution" is no longer needed if the goal is exactly the opposite, if you *want* to remember, if you want to feel your plight and to understand its reasons, if you slowly become aware of why you were so afraid of acknowledging the reasons. This can happen once you decide to stop running away, to stop betraying yourself, to allow the truth to enter your consciousness. You decide to do so because you finally no longer want to watch your life go by before having even begun to live. You decide to stop betraying yourself because you understand that only you can give yourself the love and care you never received and that you can't do that as long as you deny the truth.

Fortunately, the number of therapists who are trained in the new methods is now growing.

The more familiar you become with your biography, the better you will have learned to perceive your internal signals and take them seriously, and the easier you can judge whether your therapists follow along with you and help you or whether they only serve to confuse you more. If you don't want to pay the bill for someone else's confusion, you must have the strength and the wisdom to give up a therapist or a confusing group as you would give up a mechanic who politely but blindly tried to fix your car while ignoring and wanting to ignore what was really wrong in the first place. He may be a nice person but as long as he can damage you, your life may be in danger. It is, then, your life that must have priority and nothing else.

—Alice Miller
1992

APPENDIX A

*Wars and Dictators**

CHILDREN WHO HAVE BEEN BEATEN, HUMILI-ated, and abused, and who find no witness to come to their aid often develop a grave syndrome in later life: they have no knowledge of their true feelings, fear them like the plague, and are therefore incapable of recognizing vital connections. Without realizing it—and without taking responsibility for it—they work out the horrors that they once experienced on innocent people. Like their parents before them, they regard their actions as "redemption" for others. The result is action divested of all responsibility and invested with seeming legitimation by ideology working in conjunction with boundless hypocrisy. The direct consequences are destructive, cynically inhuman actions, actions inimical to life and, in the age of technological perfection, of the gravest threat to our planet.

"We do not want to beat you. But we must. We have to beat out of you the wickedness with which you were

*This article was written in February 1991 and published in Germany, Switzerland, and Italy.

born." This is, roughly, how parents spoke to their children in Luther's time. Luther told them it was their duty to save their children from the devil and thereby turn them into good and God-fearing citizens. They believed it. What they didn't know was that Martin Luther, whose mother raised him with pitiless strictness, was, by giving his sanction to this method of bringing up children, enabling himself to maintain the illusion of having had a good and loving mother. She was, if you like, invented with the aid of repression. People believed Luther, and did not know that instead of driving the "devil" out of their innocent children, each blow they gave them was sowing the seeds of destruction in an innocent being. The more severely, the more blindly, the more often they beat them, the more wicked their children became, and, as the seed ruptured in later life, the more destructive.

Do today's parents know better? Many do, but not all, not by a long shot. Many are confirmed in their ignorance by so-called "authorities," just as they were four hundred years ago. The terms of the debate have simply changed. No one today speaks about the "devil" in connection with a child's upbringing. Instead, we talk of "genes." Some members of the media don't shrink from totally ignoring the history of the last war and the lessons that can be learned from it; they inform their readers that criminality and mental illness can be traced to genes. If a person is born with the appropriate genes, they say, then he will ipso facto, turn into Hitler, Eichmann, or Himmler—come what psychologically may.

That old chestnut—that indulging children is damaging—seems to find as many advocates today as it ever did. That, we are asked to believe, is why there are so many antisocial teenagers. Discipline, say today's so-called progressive pedagogists, is the right way to bring up polite, well-balanced adults.

Doesn't reality contradict these views? Is it really true that Hitler, Eichmann, and Himmler didn't have enough discipline? Should they have been beaten even more to ensure that they didn't become mass murderers? When posed to discipline's faithful admirers, such questions invariably go unanswered. But their ideology is not concerned with facts. Their own repressed experience gives them all the sustenance they need. There, a completely different logic holds sway in any case: the logic of repression. Because their concern is not the truth, but the avoidance of old pains, contradictions do not bother them unduly.

Every human being is born into the world without bad intentions, and with the clear, strong, and unambivalent need to maintain life, to love and to be loved. But if a child encounters hatred and lies instead of love and truth; if, instead of being cared for and protected, it is beaten, then it should be able to shout and rage to defend itself against ignorance and wickedness. That would be a healthy, natural reaction to the destructive assaults of the adult world. Such protest would save the child's psychic health and dignity, its safety, integrity, its consciousness, its responsibility, and self-esteem. But a child that has been beaten, humiliated, and neglected has no such chance. All the human creature's naturally endowed ways of maintaining its integrity remain closed to it. Protest could be its death. Nor can the organism, which is still incomplete and growing, cope with these overwhelming feelings. In order to survive, therefore, the child has in most cases no choice but to repress the memory of what has happened to her. The inordinately strong, though unwanted feelings that must accompany any injury—murderous rage; a longing for revenge; feeling threatened by the whole world—must *always* be repressed. And for a child without a helping witness, her parents are the whole world. In the child's unconscious a wish is likely to form and with time consolidate itself: the wish to destroy this whole world so that she or he can at last live.

As all these feelings remain repressed, as they may never be experienced, as the need for respect, love, and truth may never be adequately articulated, many once-damaged children choose the path of symbolic satisfaction—for example, in socially accepted forms of criminality and perversion. Armaments production, arms dealing, and ultimately, war, are ideal domains for the acting out on innocent people, and with total denial of its origins, of the murderous, repressed rage that was never allowed to be experienced.

What was previously forbidden, war suddenly permits. A foe's image suffices as a target for the hate that has remained pent up for years, for the child's blind, boundless, murderous feelings—feelings that were never consciously experienced and consequently could be neither corrected nor controlled—to be unloaded in acceptable forms. In the process, these feelings need not, for a moment, penetrate consciousness.

An American fighter pilot in the Gulf War, for instance, asked how he felt when he got back from his bombing mission, said: "Great. I did my job well." Is that all? The journalist wanted to know, "What else?" The soldier responded with surprise. If this man had been able to feel, if his feelings had not been frozen in him for a long time, he would have shared the fear, powerlessness, and anger of the people he was bombing. Perhaps he would thereby have felt his own powerlessness, his defenselessness in the face of the incursions committed by adults seething with anger. Then he would have been able to see the connections between humiliations experienced early in life and the satisfaction he got from no longer being a helpless victim, but being able to threaten others with bombs. He would no longer be an ideal soldier, but a conscious person who could help others see through the mad machine whose moving parts they have unconsciously become. He could have played his part in preventing wars. Unfortunately, wars continue to be accepted, for there are so many people who have learned only to destroy life and be destroyed by others, people who were never able to develop their love of life because they were never given the chance.

What we are today witnessing is the consequence of the repression of the suffering inflicted on us in our early life, the splitting off of our feelings and the resultant blindness to vital connections. That can be clearly seen in the example of the production of chemical warfare agents. Who wanted war? German firms who produced and marketed poison gas just wanted to make a fast buck. That's legitimate, isn't it? It is also legitimate to feel nothing in the process and to ignore the consequences of our actions. That's how computers can help us. Eichmann, in fact, even managed it without one. He only had to deal with dots and dashes, not human eyes, hands, and hearts. Did the government wish poison gas to be produced? After all, the government wasn't earning anything from such a venture, though it did tolerate the good tax-payers. But that's legitimate enough. What? No one knew that one day the poison gas could be used to kill people? No. No one was responsible for such thoughts. Each person had his or her own department, and there was no "Department of Unnecessary Thoughts." But hadn't the Belgian professor Aubin Heyndric informed the United Nations and various governments about the lethal danger of poison gas production? Why did those warnings fall on deaf ears?

Today, many people are posing such questions. They invariably meet with the same answers: I didn't know. It wasn't my job. I wasn't responsible. I was just carrying out instructions. With unnerving similarity, one is reminded of the answers given after World War Two. Fifty years ago, entire peoples were slaughtered with poison gas, dubbed "a clean solution" at the time because no blood was spilled in the process. Today, children who never dared take a hard look at their fathers' deeds are involved in a possible repetition of those deeds, because, in principle, they never really questioned them. Had they done so, the hideous nature of those deeds would have been immediately apparent to them and they would never have been able to continue them.

That is the logic of repression: I refuse to know what my parents did to me and to others. I want to forgive them and not to condemn them. I don't want to question them. They are my parents, and therefore they are beyond blame. Because my system (my body) knows what happened, even though my consciousness has no memory of it as long as my feelings remain blocked, I am compelled to repeat the crimes carried out against me (the destruction of life) without realizing it. The mistreatment of my own children, horrific wars against supposed enemies, the destruction of life wherever I see it growing, allow me to raise a monument to my parents and retain my blindness.

Millions of once-humiliated, injured children, who were never allowed to defend themselves against the invasion of their integrity committed by their parents, will be reminded by the recent war of the history of their own private vulnerability. Until now they have managed to keep it more or less at bay. Now, they feel stirred up and confused. But as they lack their early memories and the feelings appropriate to them, they also lack a perspective in which to view these events. In their flight from their own painful personal history, they resort to the one means they learned as children: destroy and/or let yourself be destroyed or mistreated, but remain blind at all costs.

To keep secret from themselves their own history of painful humiliation, sold to them as a sign of love, men go to prostitutes and pay for beatings that they then tell themselves—as their parents once convinced them—they enjoy. In order to at last forget the sexual abuse of their fathers, women become prostitutes and allow themselves to be further humiliated, clinging to the old illusion that men's malleability might somehow give them power. The sex industry, with its numerous flagellant clubs, sadomasochism, and well-developed network of advertising, lives solely from this need, the need of men *and* women, to at last consign the story of their own childhood to oblivion with the help of a new, but very similar, scenario in the present.

Wars, through destruction and self-destruction, afford the ultimate opportunity to finally rid ourselves of the emotional pressure built up in us since childhood. On television recently, members of an American elite corp could be seen being instructed in the different kinds of torture they might face if captured. These "toughening-up" routines were reminiscent of the sadistic practices of Dr. Schreber,* who by all accounts also did such things "for the good of" his children, recommending them to others throughout the world. There were also women in this elite corp. All of them were volunteers. When one realizes that all those who volunteered for the Vietnam War, as studies on the Green Berets have shown, came from brutalizing backgrounds, then it is hardly surprising that men and women will let themselves be tortured of their own free will so that later, faced with *possible* torture, they will be able to

*I quoted extensively from the writing of this famous pedagogist of the nineteenth century in *For Your Own Good*.

remain hard and insensitive. Were these sons and daughters able to have access to their own, real story, they would, instead of toughening themselves, seek and find productive ways of defending the world from war.

Even the most sophisticated weapons will not put an end to the production of new weapons. Nor will they free us of hatred as long as this hatred is projected onto others and not allowed to be felt and experienced in its original context. If we wish to protect life on this planet, we can do so by questioning the present dangerous and ubiquitous blindness—above all, as it exists within ourselves. Human beings who know their histories will not want to sacrifice their lives so that other people can settle old scores, and they will have no difficulty finding other ways of existing and resolving conflicts than war. If our planet is indeed to have a better chance of survival, there is no alternative to the truth—by which I mean confronting ourselves with our individual and collective history.

February 1991

APPENDIX B

A Law Against the Business of Tyranny

*THE MAIN PRINCIPLE GOVERNING TRADI*tional upbringing, still widely practiced and today even increasingly advocated, differs little from that current in Luther's day. Essentially parents say: "We must make you unhappy today so that God may love you tomorrow." Drawing on numerous shocking examples, Philip Greven has described in his book, *Spare the Child* (Knopf, 1991), how this attitude has managed to persist until today.

Such an attitude effectively authorizes parents to regard the mistreatment of children as a valid way of child rearing—"for your own good." They engender in their children a blindness to hypocrisy that often has disastrous political consequences. It is quite natural that, in order to survive, children who have been mistreated and misled repress their agony. When they do not learn that this repression can later be resolved and when no one helps them to call into question the cruelty of their upbringing, they continue to perpetuate this tradition as adults. By creating further cruelty, they protect themselves from the pain of the truth.

The principle "I am beating you for your own good. One day you will thank me for it" can thus be found in the careers of all dictators, regardless of religion or culture. They call themselves the redeemers and saviors of their people, causing their subjects immense, unnecessary suffering, apparently in order to help them. In reality, they are seeking to ward off the humiliations, threats, and anxieties of their own childhood. By holding hostage the world around them, by humiliating, blackmailing, and torturing their fellow human beings, they attempt to turn the tables on their past: *they* now perpetrate the terror, disguising it as philanthropy, just as their parents once did.

Why, though, do such people succeed? Why do so many people take empty, hypocritical speeches at face value? The answer is that they have never obviously come into contact with anything else. To distinguish a lie from the truth one must have had the experience of honesty and responsibility. Unfortunately, there are millions of people who have never had this experience. They believe in the false "Redeemer" and are willing to follow him even to the gates of hell.

Napoleon's inner logic forced him to constantly try to prove, through victories, the worth that he had struggled, unsuccessfully, to gain as a child. He promised the French "La Grande Nation," and brought them eventually the misery and pain of the campaign in Russia. Nevertheless, the French people are still proud of him.

Stalin banished millions of people ostensibly to free the Soviet Union of its "inner enemies." In reality it was his own drunken father, the father who had mercilessly beaten him as a child, from whom he vainly sought to free himself. For a number of years, his persecution mania found a convenient alibi in the real political necessity of defending his country against Hitler's invasion, but as soon as the war was over, the maniacal persecution of his supposed enemies began again. No measure, though, could succeed in pacifying his panic-stricken fear, a fear that had its roots in his childhood. As long as it remained at the level of unconsciousness, as long as it was not permitted to be experienced in its real context, this fear remained hermetically sealed and unresolvable, a motor continually driving the despot to ever new crimes.

The same is true of Adolf Hitler, who was treated like a dog by his father and, like a dog, whipped by him from an early age. Hitler was proud of the fact that he had been manly enough to even count the strokes he received and feel nothing in the process. This total suppression of all feeling enabled him, with the help of repression, to survive his childhood and to continue to hold his father in great esteem. What he didn't know was that, as he murdered millions of innocent people, he was in fact attempting to annihilate that father. But nothing could finally relieve him of his rage and repressed pain. In the will that he framed only days before his death, Hitler urged his followers on to further killing, because repressed hatred is by its nature insatiable.

Nicolae Ceausescu was deposed before he had time to send his nation to war in order to "save" them. But he did reenact the scenario of his own childhood, by inflicting it on the Rumanian people with a precision that only the unconscious is capable of. For twenty years, the misery, hunger, coldness, fear, and, above all, the hypocrisy that he had repressed were inflicted on a whole nation. And this, *only because a single individual refused to confront his own personal history*.

People, mistreated as children, who live in ignorance of their own story, are easily misled. To their ears, the absurd notion that God Himself legitimates the megalomania of their rulers does not ring with absurdity. How often did they hear, as children, that God was working his purpose out in the harsh punishment meted out to them? In their experience, God was always on the side of the powerful. And as grown-up children they are therefore willing to die for the insane projects of dictators, believing that this death is as necessary to God as the punishment inflicted on "bad" children.

Wars and mistreatment of children are not specific to any one culture. They have existed, and continue to exist, the world over. There are probably only a very few cultures in which the mistreatment of children—and significantly enough, also wars—are unknown—cultures in which children are raised with great respect, and therefore accumulate no rage in their unconscious. In our society, by contrast, the physical abuse of children is still not illegal; thus, leaders who condemn others to misery and commit mass crimes, can still be celebrated as heroes. For thousands of years, infanticide was allowed, and it is not so long ago that it was made illegal. It takes time to recover from our cruel traditions. But the effects of the mistreatment of children—the repetition of violence and the universal blindness—leave us with little time.

The destructive business of tyranny can only be stopped once there is an international law that unequivocally condemns such actions as criminal and persecutes them, because a dictator, on his own, will change his strategies but never his goal, which constantly drives him to destruction until his death. Thus, this law must, categorically and effectively, deny him the freedom to go on murdering and torturing other people. People who live in a totalitarian system cannot free themselves from tyrants. They absolutely need help from the outside world, from an international law that would protect them. Ceausescu was able to inflict untold suffering on millions of women and men for twenty years without fear of indictment and to live as a respected member of the international community. This state of affairs could have been changed much earlier if an appropriate international law had existed.

A new law, however, must be accompanied by a desire to learn about the origins of tyranny. We must see how accurately violence experienced in childhood is perpetuated in the political arena because ultimately this mechanism, supported by our ignorance, is the invisible capital that finances all tyranny's ventures.

Crimes of tyrants are not natural disasters. We *can* and *must* avoid them.

APPENDIX C

A Letter to Alice Miller

TO: Miss Alice Miller, author of For Your Own Good.

Dear Mrs. Miller,

I wanted to drop you a quick line to express my gratitude for your book *For Your Own Good*. It was a revelation, one of those books that endures in the mind and helps us to "make sense" of the world.

I attached a copy of an article from a small magazine I receive that contains a comment that bears uncanny resemblance to the "poisonous pedagogy" you excoriate. The magazine is published by Dallas Theological Seminary, Dallas, Texas. This particular article was published in the Winter 1990 issue.

This is not, of course, to disparage Dallas Seminary; they are a highly respected school for Christian ministers and much of what they publish is sensible and beneficial. But this comment caught my eye. I had just finished reading your book and the coincidence was too startling to keep to myself. The question that immediately arises after reading the gentleman's comment is: How does making a child unhappy make him good? Why are the two—unhappiness and goodness—logically connected? Surely, if "being good" means being kind, sensitive to the needs of others and, above all, loving, then what better way to ensure just the opposite outcome than by "making your child unhappy" which can only make the child angry, frustrated and confused?

Anyway, before I get carried away and get in over my head explicating your book, I'd like to thank you once again for your work.

Sincerely,

Robert S.

The quotation mentioned in Robert S.'s letter reads as follows:

> *God has priorities just like we do. Sometimes in order to bring to pass something of greater importance God forgoes something else of lesser importance. Every responsible parent does the same thing. A good father, for example, wants his children to be happy. But he will make them unhappy by disciplining as needed in order to accomplish something more important, namely making them good people.*

APPENDIX D

Ten Reasons Not to Hit Your Kids by Jan Hunt

1. The practice of hitting children teaches them to become hitters themselves. Extensive research data is now available to support the direct correlation between corporal punishment in childhood and violent behavior in the teenage and adult years. Virtually all of the most dangerous criminals were regularly threatened and punished in childhood.

2. Punishment gives the message that "might makes right," that it is okay to hurt someone smaller and less powerful than you are. The child then feels it is appropriate to mistreat younger or smaller children, and when he becomes an adult, feels little compassion for those less fortunate or powerful than he is, and fears those who are more so. Thus it is difficult for him to find meaningful friendships.

3. Children learn best through parental modelling. Punishment gives the message that hitting is an appropriate way to express one's feelings and to solve problems. If the child rarely sees the parent handle anger

and solve problems in a creative and positive way, he can never learn how to do that himself. Thus inadequate parenting continues into the next generation.

4. The oft-quoted "spare the rod and spoil the child" is in fact a misinterpretation of biblical teaching. Although the rod is mentioned many times in the Bible, it is only in the Book of Proverbs (the words of King Solomon) that it is used in connection with child rearing. Solomon's methods worked very badly for his own son, Prince Rehoboam. In the Bible, there is no support for hitting children outside of Solomon's Proverbs. Jesus saw children as being close to God and urged love, not punishment.

5. Punishment greatly interferes with the bond between parent and child, as no human being feels loving toward someone who deliberately hurts him. The true cooperative behaviour the parent desires can only be accomplished through a strong bond based on loving feelings, and through many examples of kindness and cooperative skills. Punishment, even when it appears to work, can produce only superficially "good" behaviour based on fear.

6. Anger which cannot be safely expressed becomes stored inside; angry teenagers do not fall from the sky. Anger that has accumulated for many years can come as a shock to parents whose child now feels strong enough to express this rage. Thus punishment may produce "good behaviour" in the early years, but at a high price, paid by the parent and society, during adolescence and adulthood.

7. Spanking on the buttocks, an erogenous zone during early childhood, can lead to an association of

pain and erotic pleasure, causing sexual difficulties in adulthood.

8. Spanking can be physically damaging. Blows to the lower end of the spinal column send shock waves the length of the column, and may cause subdural hematoma. The prevalence of lower back pain among adults may have its origins in early corporal punishment. Paralysis has occurred through nerve damage, and children have died after relatively mild paddlings, due to undiagnosed medical problems. Many parents are unaware of alternative approaches to try, so that when punishment doesn't accomplish the parent's goals, it escalates, easily crossing the line into child abuse.

9. In many, if not most cases of "bad behaviour," the child is responding to neglect of basic needs: proper sleep and nutrition, treatment of hidden allergies, fresh air, exercise, freedom to explore the world around him, etc. But his greatest need is for his parents' undivided attention. In these busy times, few children receive sufficient time and attention from their parents, who are often too tired and distracted to treat their children with patience and understanding. Punishing a child for responding in a natural way to having had important needs neglected, is really unfair.

10. Perhaps the most important problem with punishment is that it distracts the child from the problem at hand, as he becomes preoccupied with feelings of anger and revenge. In this way the child is deprived of the best opportunities for learning creative problem-solving, and the parent is deprived of the best opportunities for letting the child learn moral values as they relate to real situations. Thus punishment teaches a child nothing about how to handle similar situations in the future.

Loving support is the only way to learn true moral behaviour based on strong inner values rather than superficially "good" behaviour based only on fear.

Strong inner values can only grow in freedom, never under fear (see Appendix C).

—reprinted by permission of EPPOCH
(End Physical Punishment of Children)
by Jan Hunt

Bibliography

ALEXANDER, THERESA. *Facing the Wolf.* New York: Dutton, 1996.

BIELER, MANFRED. *Quiet as Night.* Hamburg: Hoffmann und Campe, 1989.

DAVIS, GLENN. *Childhood and History in America.* New York: Psychohistory Press, 1976.

FEST, JOACHIM C. *Hitler.* Berlin: Propyläen, 1973.

FLIESS, ROBERT. *Symbol, Dream and Psychosis.* New York: International University Press, 1973.

GREVEN, PHILIP. *Spare the Child.* New York: Knopf, 1991.

HÖSS, RUDOLF. *Der Kommandant von Auschwitz.* Ed. by Martin Broszat. Munich: DTV, 1963.

JENSON, JEAN, M.S.W. *Reclaiming Your Life.* New York: Dutton, 1995; Meridian, 1996.

LIGHTFOOT-KLEIN, HANNY. *Prisoners of Ritual.* New York: Harrington Park Press, 1989.

MILLER, ALICE. *The Drama of the Gifted Child.* London: Virago Press, 1984; New York: Basic Books, 1980, 1997.

———. *For Your Own Good.* New York: Farrar, Straus and Giroux, 1982; London: Virago Press, 1984.

———. *Thou Shalt Not Be Aware.* New York: Farrar, Straus and Giroux, 1984; London: Pluto Press, 1984; U.S. paperback, New York: Meridian, 1991.

———. *Pictures of a Childhood.* New York: Farrar, Straus and Giroux, 1985; Meridian, 1995.

———. *The Untouched Key.* New York: Doubleday, 1990a; London: Virago Press, 1990; paperback, New York: Anchor Press, 1991a.

———. *Banished Knowledge.* New York: Doubleday, 1990b; London, Virago Press, 1990; paperback, New York: Anchor Press, 1991b.

MITHERS, CAROL LYNN. *Therapy Gone Mad.* Reading, Mass.: Addison-Wesley, 1994.

NEWELL, PETER. *Children Are People, Too.* London: Bedford Square Press, 1989.

PACEPA, ION. *Horizons Rouges.* Paris: Presse de la Cité, 1987.

SIEGERT, HEINZ. *Ceausescu: Management für das moderne Rumänien.* Munich: Bertelsmann, 1973.

TEMOSHOK, LYDIA, AND HENRY DREHER. *The Type C Connection.* New York: Random House, 1992; Plume, 1993.

TOLAND, JOHN. *Adolf Hitler.* Lübbe: Bergisch-Gladbach, 1977.

WALKER, PETE. *The Tao of Fully Feeling.* Lafayette, Calif.: Azure Coyote, 1995.

WISECHILD, LOUISE. *The Obsidian Mirror.* Seattle: Seal Press, 1988.

Index

Abortion:
  religious beliefs and, 141–43
  in Rumania, 100, 107
Abraham, 59
Academia, attitude toward child abuse, 22–23
Adam and Eve, 123
Addiction, viii, 2, 13, 129, 152, 154
  to alcohol, viii, 13–14, 17, 95, 98, 130, 152
  to drugs, viii, 130, 145, 152, 154
Adler, Alfred, 30
Adlerians, 46
Adolf Hitler (Toland), 85
African women, removal of clitorises of, 73–75
AIDS, 130, 139
Alcohol addiction, viii, 13–14, 17, 95, 98, 130, 152
Anger, 34, 36, 49, 61, 152, 174–75
  acted out on children, 36, 61–63, 73–74
  control of, 32
  justifiable, 38
  repressed, 73–74
Animals:
  behavior of, 80
Armaments:
  merchants, 161
  production of, 161
Artistic freedom, 88
Aryans, 87
Autism, 46–47
Aztecs, 88

Balint, Michael, 43
Banished Knowledge (Miller), 57, 58, 61, 75, 79, 113, 144
Beating of children, 157–59, 173,
  as accepted behavior, 51–52, 90, 96, 102–03
  legislation prohibiting, 63, 83, 143–48, 168
  as tradition, 77
  who became tyrants, *see* Ceausescu, Nicholae; Hitler, Adolf; Stalin, Joseph
  see also Child abuse
Beckett, Samuel, 114
Bible, 114–15

Bible *(cont'd)*
  Lamentations of Jeremiah, 115–21, 122, 124–25
Bieler, Manfred, 64–65
Blame, placing, on parents, 36
Body language, 98

Cancer, 138, 153
Cannibalism, 89
Castle, The (Kafka), 113
Catholic Church, 141, 143
Ceausescu, Andruza, 95, 97, 107
Ceausescu, Elena, 106, 108
Ceausescu, Nicolae, 26, 82, 94–111, 141, 146, 167, 168–69
  as abused child, 95–96, 98–101, 103–06
  imprisonment of, 104
  lack of information about childhood of, 96–98, 103–105
  need for recognition, 105–06
  as paranoid, 108
  sibling with same name, 97, 105
Ceausescu (Siegert), 96–97
Central Europe, 81
Chaplin, Charlie, 95
Chemical weapons, 161
Child abuse:
  abused as abuser, 3–4, 123
  academia's attitude toward, 22–23
  as a crime, 35–36, 49, 56, 68, 137–38, 146, 168
  as custom or tradition, 73–77, 90, 139–40, 165
  defenselessness of children, 113, 114
  destruction resulting from, *see* Destructive use of power
  expressed in literature, 112–14
  facing truth of, *see* Truth of your childhood
  ignoring of child as a person, 19–22
  infamous victims of, *see names of individuals*
  as invisible, 112
  legislation prohibiting, 63, 83, 143–48, 168
  media and, 5, 14–17, 18, 54–69
  perpetuation of lies of, 51
  prevalence of, 69
  psychiatrists and, *see* Psychiatrists; Therapy
  psychic, 64, 90, 93
  public support for corporal punishment, 51, 90, 96, 103
  "redemptive" motive for, *see* Redemption
  religion and, *see* Religion
  remembering the abuse, 33–34
  repression of memories of, *see* Repression
  self-destructive behavior and, *see* Self-destructive behavior
  sexual, *see* Child sexual abuse
  tyrants produced by, *see* Tyrants; *names of individuals*
  as unpunished crime, 84
  wall of silence around, 25, 54, 147
Child murder, 16, 76, 114, 168
Child protection agencies, 84, 90, 123
Child rearing, 114, 138, 139, 146
  abusive, *see* Child abuse
  cruel, 76, 89, 144–45, 158, 162
  in Germany, 79, 80–81, 83–84, 86–87, 90–92
  language of traditional, 109
  psychic abuse under guise of, 64
Children Are People, Too (Newell), 145

Child sexual abuse, 6–9, 150–51, 163
- abused as abuser, 3–4
- facing truth of, 8–9
- in Germany, 5–6
- media treatment of, 5, 14–17, 18
- mother's role in, 7–8, 133–34
- statistics, 68
- wall of silence around, 5–6, 9, 18, 19

China, binding of girls' feet in, 77
Chronic illness, 138
Clitoris, removal of, 73–76
Collective unconscious, 29
Communism, 100, 122
Communist Party of Rumania, 96, 104
Creativity, destruction of, 86
Criminal behaviour:
- child abuse as, 35–36, 49, 56, 68, 138, 146
- as apparently genetically determined, 158
- resulting from child abuse, 130, 145, 147

Custom:
- circumcision as, 75–76
- clitoridectomy as, 73–75, 76
- *see also* Tradition

Dallas Theological Seminary, 171
"Daughters Are Breaking Their Silence," 5–6
Denial, 2, 7, 82, 83, 84, 85, 114, 122, 137, 150
- *see also* Repression

Depression, 3,
Destructive use of power, vii, viii, 61, 79, 82, 92, 93, 106–107, 160, 162
- in the Bible, 114
- by Ceausescu, *see* Ceausescu, Nicolae
- by Hitler, *see* Hitler, Adolf
- redemption through, 102–103, 108, 109–10, 157–58, 166
- by Stalin, *see* Stalin, Joseph
- wars, *see* Wars

Dictators, *see* Tyrants
Discipline, abusive, *see* Child abuse
Disobedience, *see* Obedience
Doctors, 55, 58, 124, 139
Drama of the Gifted Child, The (Miller), 55, 57, 59
Drug addiction, viii, 130, 145, 152, 154

Eastern Europe, 81
Eichmann, Adolf, 158, 159, 161
Electroshock therapy, 32, 34
Eltern, 56
Empathy, 18, 26, 56, 113
- inability to feel, 85, 105

Enemas, 8
England, 47, 144, 145
Enlightened witnesses, 17, 51, 67, 69, 81, 83, 129,
- of Bieler, 64, 65
- as safety net for children, 136–37

EPPOCH (End Physical Punishment of Children), 17, 144–45
Erickson, Milton H., 48
"Established Knowledge," 59
Euthanasia legislation of Third Reich, 64, 101,
Eve, 13–18

Facing the Wolf (Alexander), 48*n.*
Fairy tales, 113
Fanaticism, 122
Fascism, 24, 81–83, 86
Fathers, 112
- absolute obedience to, 87, 89
- child abuse by, *see* Child abuse
- mother siding with, 87

Fathers *(cont'd)*
  tyrant as father figure, 56
  see also Parents
Feelings, therapeutic importance of, 138, 164
Ferenczi, Sandor, 43, 49
Fest, Joachim, 78, 94
"Final Solution," 64
Finland, 144
Flaubert, Gustave, 114
Fliess, Robert, 43, 49
Forgetting the abuse, therapy based on, 32, 33, 36, 39–40, 134
Forgiveness, 35, 55, 115, 162
  therapy based on, 33, 36, 46, 123, 130–36, 137
For Your Own Good (Miller), 41, 79, 86, 94, 101, 151*n.*, 171–72
France, 144–45, 166
Freedom, 81
Freud, Sigmund, 30, 45, 151
  disciples of, 43–44
  suppression of truth of child abuse, 43, 61, 151
  challengers of, 42–43
Front National, French, 103

Genocide, 89
German Society for Child Protection, 123
Germany, 5–6, 17, 18, 43, 144, 145, 161
  Berlin wall, 141
  Catholic Church in, 141
  child abuse in, 58, 59
  childrearing in, 79, 80–81, 83–84, 86–87, 90–91, 92
  child sexual abuse in, 5–6
  Third Reich, *see* Hitler, Adolf; Nazis; Nazism
God, 124 167–68, 172
  of Creation, 123
  unpredictable, 115
Good and evil, distinguishing between, 122–23
Gorbachev, Mikhail, 146
Great Britain, 47, 144, 145
Green Berets, 80, 163
Guilt:
  of abused, 20, 22, 35, 115, 122, 124, 129–30, 132, 145
  in psychoanalysis, 45
Gulf War, vii, 160
Gypsies, 87

Handicapped, 88
Hatred, 58, 131
  acting out, 58, 82, 91, 167
  experiencing feeling of, 58–59, 91
Hauptmann, Gerhard, 86
Heidegger, Martin, 86
Heyndric, Aubun, 161
Himmler, Heinrich, 158, 159
Hitler, Adolf, 25–26, 62, 78–93, 106, 141, 146, 159
  as abused child, 25–26, 64–65, 79, 85–86, 90, 95, 159, 167
  acting out hatred, 58, 167
  ancestry of father of, 102
  attempts to wipe out his past, 106
  euthanasia legislation, 64, 101
  "Final Solution," 64
  German childrearing and Nazism, 86–88, 92
  invasion of Russia, 166
  lack of empathy, 85
Hitler (Fest), 78, 94
Hitler's Childhood (Radström), 63–64
Höss, Rudolf, 80–81
Hölderlin, Friedrich, 29
"Holding" therapy, 46–47
Holocaust, 39, 40
Homosexuals, 87
Hope, 138

Horizons Rouges (Pacepa), 98, 110
Human sacrifice, 88
Hunger Artist, The (Kafka), 113
Hypnosis, 1, 152

Immune system, 139
Indulging of children, viii, 158
Infanticide, 114, 168
Infant mortality in Rumania, 97
Insulin, 32
International law, 158
International Psychoanalytic Association, 43
Isaac, 59
Isolation, feeling of, 50

Jeremiah, Lamentations of, 115–21, 122, 124
Jews, 87, 101, 141
  circumcision, 75–76
Jones, Ernest, 43
Jung, Carl, 30
Jungians, 44

Kafka, Franz, 19, 62, 113
Kohut, Heinz, 49
Kommandant von Auschwitz, Der (Höss), 80

Lamentations of Jeremiah, 115–21, 122, 124
Laws prohibiting
  child abuse, 62, 83, 143–66, 168
  tyranny, 165–69
Legislation prohibiting
  child abuse, 63, 83, 143–66, 168
  tyranny, 165–69
Lightfoot-Klein, Hanny, 73
Literature, child abuse expressed in, 112–14
  Bible, *see* Bible
Long Day's Journey into Night, A, 112–13
LSD, 1
Luther, Martin, 158, 165

Mandalas, 30
Manipulative therapies, 46, 47
Marxist-Leninism, *see* Communism
Mause, Lloyd de, xiv, 23
Media, 150
  treatment of subject of child abuse in, 5, 14–17, 18, 54–69
Medical experiments on humans, 89
Medical technology, 124
Medication, 13, 30, 31, 32, 137, 139
Memories of the abuse, 33–34
  see also Repression
Mengele, Joseph, 89
Mentally ill, 88, 158
Metamorphosis (Kafka), 113
Milgram test, 89, 89*n.*
Miller, Alice (author):
  and daughter, xii–xiv
  mother's behavior toward, xii–xiii, 19–22
  programs using name of, 48
  reaction to her work on mistreatment of children, 42–43, 56, 57, 58–64, 66–67
  in therapy, 4, 9, 134, 135
  writings of, *see individual titles*
Morality, 38, 89, 96, 136, 139, 152
More Revealed (Ragge), 149*n.*
Morris, Desmond, 75
Mothering, 75
Mothers, 112–13
  abortion option, *see* Abortion
  child abuse by, *see* Child abuse
  role in child sexual abuse, 7–8, 132–33

Mothers *(cont'd)*
  siding with father, 87
  wall of silence put up by, 19–22
  see also Parents
Munch, Edvard, 29
Murder of children, 16, 76, 114, 168

Napoleon, 110, 166
Nazis, 89, 92–93, 158, 159, 161
  childhoods of, 80, 159
  Hitler, *see* Hitler, Adolf
Nazism:
  passive complicity of Germans, 91
  tenets of, 87–88
Newell, Peter, 144–45
Nietzsche, Friedrich, 27–29, 31, 38, 68
  abuse as child, 27–28, 29
  loses his mind, 29, 50
Norway, 144
Nuclear war, 91

Obedience:
  punishment for disobedience, 114
  redemption for, 114
  unquestioning, 75, 78, 81, 86, 87, 88, 89, 92
Obsidian Mirror, The (Wisechild), 132–33
Old Testament, 104, 114–15
  Lamentations of Jeremiah, 115–21, 122, 124
O'Neill, Eugene, 112

Pacepa, Ion, 98, 110
Pain, avoidance of, 27, 130, 138
  conscious experience of, 21, 48, 123, 134, 137
Parents:
  abuse by, *see* Child abuse; Child sexual abuse
  criticism of, 38
  fidelity to abusing, 95, 123
  forgiveness of, *see* Forgiveness
  love for abusing, 123
  placing blame on, 36
  understanding for abusing, 123
  unquestioning obedience to, 75, 78, 81, 86, 89
  see also Mothers; Fathers
Paris Match, 51
Pedagogy:
  of childrearing, *see* Childrearing
  of doctors, *see* Doctors
  of psychiatrists, *see* Psychiatrists
  of religion, *see* Religion
  of therapists, *see* Therapy
Penal Colony (Kafka), 19, 62, 113
Perestroika, 122
Permissiveness, 158
Physical abuse of children, *see* Beating of children; Child abuse
Physicians, 55, 124, 139
Pictures of a Childhood (Miller), xii
Poison gas, 161–162
Political ideologies:
  Communism, 99, 122
  fanaticism, 122
  fascism, 24, 81–82, 86
  seeking refuge in, 2
Post-traumatic stress syndrome, 39
Power:
  destructive use of, *see* Destructive use of power
  insecure seeking, 21
Prostitution, 163
Psychedelic drugs, 2
  LSD, 1

Psychiatrist, 27–40, 139
child abuse ignored by, 27, 30–31, 36, 48–49, 55
fear of confronting their own past, 37, 133–35
forgetting as therapy, 32, 33, 36, 39–40, 134
forgiveness as therapy, *see* Forgiveness
medication prescribed by, 30, 31, 32, 139
Psychic child abuse, 63, 90, 93
Psychoanalysis, 41–46
challengers of Freudian theory, 42–43
evasion of realities of child abuse, 41–45, 50, 123–24
example of distortions of, 44–45
guilt laid on patient in, 45
Psychosis, 130, 145
Psychotherapy, schools of, 30–31
Psychotics, 30
Punishment, 172–75

Quiet as Night: The Memoirs of a Child (Bieler), 64–65

Rädstrom, Niklas, 63
Rape, 7, 8, 132–33
Rauschning, Hermann, 85
Rebirthing, 1
Reclaiming Your Life (Jenson), x–xi, 48*n*.
Recognition, need for, 105
"Recovery from Self-Betrayal" (Miller), 149–155
Redemption, 114, 122
as apparent motive of abuse, 96
for obedience, 114
through destruction, 102–03, 108–10, 157–58, 166,
Religion, 2, 38, 122 124, 139
abortion and, 141–43
Bible, *see* Bible
child abuse in name of, 96, 98–99, 144, 167–68, 169
fanaticism, 122
human sacrifice, 88
mutilation in name of custom, 75–76
unpredictable God, 114–15
Remembering the abuse, 33–34
(see also) Repression
Repression, 15, 21, 22, 24, 28, 114, 162
of anger, *see* Anger
of child sexual abuse, 132
of pain, 27, 41, 130, 138
as child's means of survival, 50, 79, 103–105, 137–138, 149–150, 159, 165
collective, 98–99
destructive consequences of, 3–4, 82, 106, 130, 149
dispensing with, as adults, 48, 79, 105–106, 137–38, 149
violence and, 1–2
Revenge, vii, 7, 8, 74, 75, 76, 82, 83, 142, 147, 159
Ceausescu's acts of, 96, 100, 104–106
Hitler's desire for, 83
war as means of, 91
Rumania:
under Ceausescu, 95, 98–111, 141, 146, 147, 167, 168–69
infant mortality in, 97
life of peasant in, 97
population policy, 99–100, 107–108
secret police, 99, 102, 107, 110, 141
Russia, 166–67
Russians, 88

Sadism, 19, 20
sadistic newborn, 30

Sadomasochism, 163
Schrebers, Dr., 163
Sects, cults, x–xii
Securitate (Rumanian secret police), 100, 102, 107, 110, 141
Seigert, Heinz, 96–98
Self-destructive behaviour, 38, 60–61, 79
  addiction, *see* Addiction
  suicide, 13, 23
Self-help groups, 6
Sex offenders, 7
Sexual abuse of children, *see* Child sexual abuse
Sleeping disorders, 3
Sleeping pills, 3
Social consciousness, 4
Song of Solomon, 103
Soviet Union, 166–67
Spanking, 174
Spare the Child (Greven), 165
Stalin, Joseph, 82, 106, 141, 146, 166–67
  as abused child, 26, 95, 166
Stalinism, 81, 109
Statistics on child abuse, 68
Stress hormones, 137
Substance abuse, *see* Alcohol addiction: Drug addiction
Suicide, 13, 23
Suppression of truth, 66–67, 96
Sweden, 143–44, 145
Switzerland, 17, 76–77
Symbol, Dream and Psychoanalysis (Fliess), 43

Tao of Fully Feeling, The (Walker), ix–x
Teachers, beatings by, 35
Technology, 124
Temesvar, Rumania, 101
Terrorism, 145
Therapy, 13–14, 21, 123–24, 139
  "authority" of therapist, 134
  based on forgiveness, 33, 36, 46, 123–24, 130–36, 137,
Therapy Gone Mad (Mithers)
Third Reich, *see* Hitler, Adolf; Nazis; Nazism
Thou Shalt Not Be Aware (Miller), 5, 41, 42, 43, 48, 113
Thus Spoke Zarathustra (Nietzsche), 68
Toland, John, 85
Torture, 163–64
Totalitarianism, 168
Tradition, 76–77, 90, 140, 165
  see also Custom
Tranquilizers, 137
Trial, The (Kafka), 113
Truth of your childhood, 23–24, 136, 153
  fear of confronting, 66–67
  importance of facing, 2–4, 91, 137, 139, 145, 152
  repression of, *see* Repression
  sexual abuse, *see* Child sexual abuse
Type C Connection, The, (Temoshock and Dreher), 153*n*.
Tyrants, 52–53, 82, 147, 165–69
  as abused children, 25–26, 52, 147, 166
  destructive use of power, *see* Destructive use of power
  recognizing, 108–09
  as "strong father" figure, 53
  see also names of individuals, e.g. Ceausescu, Nicolae; Hitler, Adolf; Stalin, Joseph

United Nations, 161
United States, therapy in, 46–47, 131

Untouched Key, The (Miller), 27, 58, 59, 79
"Ur-situation," 114

van Gogh, Vincent, 29
Vietnam War, 39, 80, 163
Violence, 24–25, 90–91
  child abuse, *see* Child abuse
  as necessary to maintain order, 90
  repressed abuse resulting in, 1–2
  see also Destructive use of power

Wars, 77, 89, 93, 142, 160–61, 164
"Wars and Dictators" (Miller), 157–64
Weapons, *see* Armaments
Weimar Republic, 83
"Wild Water" *(Wildwasser)*, 6
Wisechild, Louise, 132–33
Women's movement, 6
  illusions concerning child sexual abuse, 7